This Pākehā Life
An Unsettled Memoir

To dear Aunt C
with love,

Alison

This Pākehā Life
An Unsettled Memoir

ALISON JONES

Bridget Williams Books

First published in 2020 by Bridget Williams Books Ltd,
PO Box 12474, Wellington 6144, New Zealand

ISBN 9781988587288 (Paperback), ISBN 9781988587257 (EPUB)
ISBN 9781988587264 (Kindle), ISBN 9781988587271 (PDF)
DOI https://doi.org/10.7810/9781988587288

Acknowledgements
The publishers would like to acknowledge the ongoing support of
the BWB Publishing Trust, which enables all BWB publications.
The commitment of Creative New Zealand to good New Zealand
publishing is also acknowledged, and its support for this
publication is appreciated.

Editorial note
Macrons are used on Māori words and terms, tribal names, place
names, names of organisations and personal names. They are not
used for source titles unless present in the original. Macrons are
used in reported speech, but in quotations only if they were in the
original source. Māori and Pacific language words are defined either
in the text on their first usage, or in the glossary. The names of
some people have been changed to protect their identities.

All reasonable efforts have been made to obtain permission,
where necessary, from copyright holders. Any omissions or errors
are unintentional and will be corrected in future printings upon
notification by relevant copyright holders.

A catalogue record for this book is available from the National
Library of New Zealand. Kei te pātengi raraunga o Te Puna
Mātauranga o Aotearoa te whakarārangi o tēnei pukapuka.

Edited by Caren Wilton
Cover and internal design by Jo Bailey
Typesetting by Tina Delceg
Printed and bound in Australia by Griffin Press, part of Ovato.

Contents

Preface

I'm keen on the idea at first. Anywhere has to be better than here. It is a Friday afternoon on a typical wet grey winter's day in Auckland. My friend and academic colleague Te Kawehau and I sit in a steamed-up café discussing the merits of a university teaching job in another country. Australia, perhaps, for warmer weather. Or England, not for the weather, but for a change. Te Kawehau is clear. She says she could not live very long outside Aotearoa New Zealand: 'This is the only place I make sense.'

Her sentiments unexpectedly reflect my own. This country has formed both of us, in different ways. As a Māori woman from the Northland hapū Ngāti Hau, she has roots here that are hundreds of years old. I am the daughter of English immigrants, a child born into this land and haunted by ghosts of foreign hills. I became who I am here. In this café, right now, I realise that I cannot imagine living anywhere else. The needle on my built-in compass would always be swivelling towards home.

This book is about my making sense here, of my becoming and being Pākehā. Every Pākehā becomes a Pākehā in their own way, finding their own meaning for that Māori word. This is the story of what it means to me. I have written this book for Pākehā – and other New Zealanders – curious about their sense of identity and about the ambivalences we Pākehā often experience in our relationships with Māori.

———

'Pākehā' is a complicated and politicised term in modern
usage. It is a tuna-term, a slippery eel of a word; it wriggles
easily away from one's grasp. Sometimes it is a general
descriptive category to name the white people inhabiting New
Zealand; sometimes it refers to an identity, a form of self-
understanding that arises from close ongoing engagement
with Māori-as-Māori. Sometimes it is used negatively by Māori
to name the colonisers. But as Ani Mikaere famously put it:
'[T]here is nowhere else in the world that one can be Pākehā.
Whether the term remains forever linked to the shameful role
of the oppressor or whether it can become a positive source
of identity and pride is up to Pākehā themselves. All that is
required from them is a leap of faith.'[1]

Many European New Zealanders have been reluctant to
take a leap and adopt this Māori name. Some have even tried
to argue, wrongly, that it is a term of abuse. Māori have been
calling Europeans 'Pākehā' ever since they first encountered
strange white beings on Captain James Cook's ship in 1769, and
the scholarly consensus seems to be that it is an ancient Māori
term with unclear origins, perhaps referring to pale, super-
natural, human-like beings.

It was not until the Pākehā historian Michael King
encouraged us in 1985 to identify ourselves as Pākehā rather
than European New Zealanders that we have been trying on
the term for size.[2] But it is still not easy to find positive modern
Pākehā histories, as the late writer Peter Wells recently pointed
out. We once were noble pioneers, settlers and colonists
about whom interesting stories could be told. Now that New
Zealand pioneers are no longer considered so noble, given their
destructive effects on Māori, Wells wrote: '[We] have been left
singularly naked, stripped of all dignity let alone identity. We

are the silhouette without a face, demoted into non-beings – we are simply "non-Māori".'[3]

I am not sure I agree. Although we are now rightly more anxious about the real and symbolic violence of New Zealand settlement, many of us do confidently take up the term Pākehā as an identity – even if its modern meaning cannot be easily pinned down, and its boundaries are unclear. Wells had a point that we rarely write in positive terms about being Pākehā, though that, too, is changing as we begin to face our relationships with Māori.

———

Michael King's motivation in 1985 to write *Being Pakeha* was his curiosity, after several years of writing about Māori, about 'who was I, who was my family, where did we come from and where did we belong?'[4] King wrote with an historian's sensibility and a certain masculine detachment: 'To be Pakeha in the 1940s and 1950s was to enjoy a way of life that changed beyond recognition in the succeeding decades. ... This book is one Pakeha's eyewitness account ... a view from the high ground of the 1980s.'[5]

My own writing in *This Pākehā Life: An Unsettled Memoir* is not so detached or confident in tone. I am not an eyewitness so much as an uncertain participant in my relationships with Māori. In this book about my becoming Pākehā, I stick close to the contours of a lifetime of personally remembered events and relationships. My modest aim in giving attention to my own everyday engagements with Māori is to give shape to one New Zealand experience of the latter half of the twentieth century.

In my recollections of becoming Pākehā I have made nothing up – at least, not knowingly – though I have discovered that some memories exist only because I want them to be true. My account of childhood relies on at least one memory that has proved ghostly – a memory that, despite being false, remains vivid, and continues to haunt me. I have changed a few names, but most people in my story have allowed me to name them, even if my memories do not always match theirs. So, inevitably, this book is also about memory, its unreliability, and how it is important to who we are.

Mine is not a redemptive story of good feelings and togetherness; I try to show that Māori–Pākehā relationships are difficult and wonderful all at once, and that such complexities are not only exciting but also make us who we are as quirkily unique New Zealanders.

Now, after more than sixty-five years of becoming Pākehā – having accepted the inevitable Pākehā state of permanent lively discomfort, and eschewing a single resolution of our relationship with Māori – I feel strangely liberated. Being Pākehā, having daily engagements with Māori-as-Māori, may not be entirely comfortable, but nor is it ever boring. For all the complexities, such relationships have given me a deeply rich sense of myself and the place I live.

———

Throughout this book I use Māori words, sometimes with a translation, sometimes allowing the context to provide meaning, though there is a glossary at the end of the book. These days it can reasonably be assumed that most New Zealanders understand the many Māori terms now used regularly in popular media such as newspapers and the radio. I like the apparently easy flow between the use of English and te reo Māori in New Zealand. At the same time, I'm cautious of depicting the casual mix of languages as unproblematic. Te reo Māori and English describe deeply different worlds. It is not a matter of simply using different words to say the same things. The fact is, key Māori words cannot be translated into a precisely equivalent English word. For instance, commonly used terms such as 'whānau' and 'whenua' are used routinely in English-language sentences to refer to 'family' and 'land' respectively. Yet to grasp their meaning in te reo Māori is to feel and understand the living links with ancestors, to recall past events, to speak of birth and death – in ways that are not at all represented by those two English words.

I could explain it another way. You get an everyday sense of different worlds when you happen upon a mundane sentence in a New Zealand short story: 'We entered the silent whare on a cold winter's night.' Whare. The word seems to arrive in the sentence from another planet. The English vowels through which you are reading are shaken up, the flow interrupted. You pause a moment and rearrange your mouth (even in your mind, with silent reading, your mind-mouth has to get itself around the words). *Whare*. The *a* is an open, short sound, you have to stretch your mouth away from the usual flat tongue of the New Zealand English speaker. Air enters the mouth, even only in the mind; you are more alert for a moment. Then the final *e* demands to be heard, and it is an odd 'e'. Not an 'ee' out of bared fangs, but a soft light sound that floats off, like the 'e' in 'egg'. The sound floats, but not vaguely – it is insistent as it rolls off the hard 'r' that sounds like a 'd', finishing the word nicely. Whare.

It's not only the sudden change in register demanded by the whare that unsettles the reader; it is not merely a matter of the strange sound of a word. The strangeness goes much further than that. If you had read 'We entered the silent hut on a cold winter's night' you would have read on, barely noticing anything except perhaps a shiver and a sense of desolation. But a whare's desolation is so much sadder and more mysterious than that of a silent room. I would barely hesitate to enter a deserted hut on a cold winter night, but a whare? Even at the doorway of a very small whare, I'd be looking out for ghosts and spirits, straight away. I'd at least peer in from the door contemplating whether to enter at all, and whether to remove my shoes as is customary for entering a whare. I would not simply walk right in.

There is something about both that shift of vowel sound and the caution at the imagined whare door that captures the disjuncture between Pākehā and Māori worlds. Some Pākehā can read the sentence, or encounter the silent whare, and make the adjustment with barely any effort. Even so, there is always some pause: the reader recognises that the word and its shape is outside of English; she feels the forces of another reality. She makes an adjustment; she cannot merely sail straight on. So, although I use Māori terms here and there in this text, I want to sound a warning against a complacent assumption of simple translations.

It is unfashionable to point to differences between humans in a modern world that aches for the basic, shared values of being (a good) human: kindness, generosity, acceptance, respect. It goes without saying, I hope, that even as cultures can and do inhabit different worlds, we are all human and we all share the higher human values. The joy of becoming Pākehā is that it requires and nurtures a *doubled being*: a sense of shared humanity with Māori as well as a deep sense of otherness, of the unknown and the unknowable. For me, it is within that fundamental tension – it's like the positive tension in a firm handshake, or a kind steady gaze between two people – that I feel truly alive, and where I make sense.

Being here

The start time was 8 a.m. and I was running late. I had
somehow failed to connect with my friends at the hotel. The
Waitangi Tribunal was holding a hearing at Waitangi and,
having done some research on the history of the north, I
was keen to listen to the local hapū histories that would be
presented at the hearing. Assuming there would be a pōwhiri, I
looked as I hurried along the Waitangi beachfront road for the
tail end of an ope, a group entering the marae. Everything would
be all right, I told myself. I would unobtrusively join the group,
and no one would realise I was late or notice I was arriving alone.
This is my default plan if I arrive at a pōwhiri by myself: I just
latch on to the latest group being welcomed on to the marae.
Having moved in the entrance as part of a larger whole, I find a
quiet spot on the sidelines, feign relaxed familiarity, survey the
scene for acquaintances and decide what to do next.

When I am anxious, I develop a sort of selective blindness,
and on this day I was very anxious. I was late and separated from
my Māori friends. I was sweaty and hot even though it was early
in the day. I had never been to a Waitangi Tribunal hearing and
I was overawed by the whole thing, even though we were in the
familiar Bay of Islands, a relaxed part of New Zealand.

The roadway along the beachfront was crowded with cars
but at last I saw what I was blindly looking for: a huddle of
people filing off the roadway into a nearby building screened

by bushy plants. The women had gone at the front, so I was among the young men at the rear. They carried flags, and a few home-made taiaha. As we reached the door I saw shoes by the steps. In a trance, I took off my own shoes and moved inside.

Inside, I scanned the place to see where I was. I was in a small room, a meeting house, painted white. It was the wharenui of Te Tii. Kids and young people were settling on the floor, and older men and women sat round the edges on benches. I was not in a Tribunal hearing. This was a small hapū group preparing themselves before giving their testimony to the Tribunal. Feeling numb with confusion and embarrassment about being there, I kept moving towards a small gap between two women about halfway along one wall. One of them shifted slightly and beckoned me. I stepped over kids and wedged myself in.

The sun was beating in hard through the windows. The adults were in black, with identical coloured scarves. I was the only Pākehā, the only stranger. No one knew who I was. Long-deceased ancestors stared into the crowd from framed drawings and photographs held on women's laps; I felt almost more aware of their black-and-white presence than of the shuffling of the living. Everyone quietened down for a karakia, intoned by an elderly man who, removing his stylish black brimmed hat, left a tuft of grey hair standing straight up from his head. Instead of bowing my head reverently, I looked for an escape route; I was not meant to be in here. I was truly jammed in, and there were many bodies between me and the crowded doorway. The woman next to me, sensing my anxiety, patted my leg with a large kind hand. Just sit, she seemed to say.

The prayer was followed by speeches and more prayers, all in Māori. The speeches were not the usual showy events, but monologues to which everyone listened in silence, even the smallest children. Sprigs of dark leaves were waved idly in the thick morning air. The ancestors were being addressed, and the land. Amongst the living, I sensed ghosts. Names and whakapapa were recited. A few people glanced at me with mild curiosity. I felt achingly conspicuous.

Then, as the minutes ticked by, something changed. I realised my presence was completely irrelevant to the event. My anxious sense of myself, and how out of place I was, missed the point. I was simply one among many. The indifference of everyone around me to my fretful presence produced in me a sudden, unfamiliar sense of calm. My self-consciousness, now meaningless, had nothing to do but dissolve. I felt myself to be simply present. I may have been seized by a sense of being in the wrong place, but there was no wrong place. The people were getting on with the job in hand, preparing themselves, mentally and spiritually, to walk with their ancestors into the huge white marquee next door to face the distinguished jurists of the Tribunal and tell their stories about how they had loved, lived on, and lost, their land.

———

I return to this memory often, sometimes as a self-mocking anecdote shared with other Pākehā worried about 'being out of place' in a Māori setting. I try to reassure them about getting it wrong: 'Well, you couldn't get dopier than me!' Sometimes I recall the sense of presence I felt in that room. My dissolving individuality, becoming part of a generous and infinitely accepting group, was a visceral experience very difficult to explain. I am normally immersed in a culture of individual embarrassment and personal choice; in that small room I could feel neither. I was simply there. I recall a sun-filled space, the upright tuft of hair, the dark green leaves, the framed portraits, and some other presence. I remember the unexpected sensation of peace.

Ghosts and arrivals

I have always been haunted by ghosts of the dead. They have haunted me subliminally, only glimpsed in decisions I have made and in my patterns of attention. I have heard that ghosts wander about, scaring human beings, causing trouble. This is not always true. My ghosts inhabit the strong positive core of me. My ghosts were present before my birth. Some came to this place with my parents, some were already here.

———

I was pushed out into a New Zealand life in September 1953, in Cornwall Park Hospital, Auckland. My mother's postnatal recovery was eased, she said rather grandly, by a view of 'a lovely emerald-green hill'. Outside her hospital window, One Tree Hill's grassy flanks rose above the city, topped by a solitary pine tree that leaned away from the westerly winds like a solidified flag. Being born in its shadow, I would always call that hill *my mountain*. Auckland became *my town*, and New Zealand *my home*. These places and their histories would form me.

Born into a life stream over which we have little control, we are carried along by our own genetic code, our gender, our parents' social class and race and education, our geographical location, and our particular period in social history. My being a girl with averagely educated white immigrant parents in New

Zealand during the post-war boom years created – with no input from me – my life's contours.

I could so easily have been formed elsewhere. It could have been Canada, or South Africa or Australia. Of all the countries advertising in English cities for young immigrants, New Zealand caught my father's eye. His wife, my mother, keen on a new life, had come with him. So here I was: bloodily pushed and dragged into New Zealand with no say in the matter. My ghosts claimed me then, but I did not know which ones until a lot later.

―――――

With no relatives here, my parents and I were alone in New Zealand. My handsome, talented father, Basil, had left his working-class family in the industrial north of England, aged twenty-six. His engineer father, like his father before him, was a 'time served' engineer, who had grown up during the great era of English colonial rule and had worked physically hard in the armaments and shipbuilding industries, serving his apprenticeship in engine rooms on steamships around the coasts of India and the Far East. He was self-conscious about his lack of education, and impressed on his two sons the benefits of education and a white-collar job. 'Don't be like me,' he urged. 'Get a job in an office, with a pension.' My father was unsuited to office work; he had a precocious talent for electronics and loved being outdoors. He was called up for National Service just as the war ended; he became adept at Morse code, and worked on the development of radar to detect submarines. But, being sensitive and anxious, he took his father's advice and trained to be an accountant.

By the war's end, Basil had decided to emigrate. Advertisements and films promoting New Zealand had enchanted him since he was twenty years old. The New Zealand National Film Unit's films *Journey for Three* and *Meet New Zealand* showed an attractive open country where a man could breathe, have his own fruit trees and keep a few bees. It was a familiar-looking place, despite its distance from Britain. The indigenous people would welcome him; the film *Aroha: A Story of the Māori People*, in which Aroha's father's illness was cured by an English doctor, suggested that the cheerful Māori people were grateful for the advanced skills of English immigrants.

Basil had been interviewed in Newcastle for a job as a clerk at the Bank of New Zealand's Queen Street branch, Auckland. He proved exactly what they wanted: young, white, educated – and soon to be married. The bank would pay Basil's fare.

My mother, aged twenty-five when I was born, came from the south of England. She had spent her life in the village of Hockley in Essex. Born illegitimately in 1928, she was abandoned at the local orphanage by her mother at ten days old with a dramatic note: 'Her name is Ruth.' I do not know if there really was such a note, but this is the story I grew up with. She was a smart and determined girl, permanently and deeply troubled by her lack of parents or any explanation of her origins, and it was she who brought many ghosts into our family.

Like a lot of bright girls at the time, my mother was deemed to be 'secretarial material', so she became a shorthand typist, topping her class in Pitman shorthand. Although she had lived in the orphanage all of her childhood, her birth mother (we found out later) had secretly paid for her to go to a 'good' school, rather than the regular village school. At eighteen, she left the orphanage and joined the Women's Royal Naval Service, swapping one institutional life for another.

Basil and Ruth met at an armed forces social event in Cardiff in Wales. My father fell immediately for the vivacious young southerner, and she was flattered. But he told her they could not get serious because he was planning to emigrate. Ruth did not hesitate: 'If we do get serious, I will come with you!' she told him. They married in 1950, and made plans to leave England for the other side of the world.

———

Basil considered Ruth better than him, not least because her southern-England accent marked her as from a higher social class. Basil's working-class family lived in a long row of identical two-storeyed brick terrace houses that opened directly onto the street. His mother scrubbed her stone doorstep every morning. When Basil took his fiancée home to meet his parents, he begged his family to 'behave in front of Ruth'. His brother remembers him going in to the kitchen during a visit to berate his mother for licking the spoon after scraping the remains of a rice pudding from its dish, and his anxiety about a broken light fitting that Ruth might notice. Basil might have been impressed with Ruth, but his parents did not take kindly to her, an outsider from the south. For her part, Ruth considered her new mother-in-law a narrow-minded and triflingly class-conscious housewife.

His parents could not persuade Basil to get work in Newcastle and live nearby. Basil could have got an office job, and a semi-detached house with a small backyard, near his parents. But in the aftermath of the bruising world war, Newcastle was a depressing, polluted place, and post-war food rationing would remain in place for years. Neither he nor Ruth had any desire to stay.

My father's distraught parents would never fully recover from the shock of his departure. His family loved their ancestral Northumberland, and found his leaving a confusing betrayal: their beloved son was taking the equivalent of a one-way trip to the outer universe, with an unsuitable woman.

———

I don't know if my father's leaving England led to what would become his defining illness. But at some point, early on, he developed an intensifying depression that would hang like a spectre – perhaps more like a guillotine – over my childhood. Maybe it was genetic; I, too, would feel the pull of depressive anxiety in later life. It is hard to know when people's personal problems begin to solidify. Was Basil's malaise a result of his decision to work in an office, when he craved the open air? Driven by guilt about leaving his parents? Or was it provoked by his marriage to my mother, a quick, outward-looking, judgmental woman whom he loved and feared in equal measure?

My mother, with little inkling of her new husband's demons and with nothing to lose, cheerfully turned her back on a parentless life, and the couple boarded a crowded ship, a former troop carrier named SS *Tamaroa*. Their departure had been delayed by trouble on the wharves at Auckland, which effectively closed New Zealand to shipping (a labour conflict still known bitterly as the 1951 waterfront lockout), so it was not until early 1952 that they finally got away.

Photographs taken on board show a happy, attractive couple on deck, basking in sunlight and expectation. Aside from their respective phantoms – my mother's lack of parents and my anxious father's desertion of his – they travelled lightly, with few keepsakes. My mother had no family objects, though in her handbag, carefully folded, was a mysterious fragment of brown paper with a London address that would later provide a clue to her origins. My father carried his father's thick leather briefcase, his grandfather's ebony and ivory domino set in its plain wooden box, a hollow green glass rolling pin, and some English china, a wedding present from his mother. Unencumbered by the past, they thought, they would make a brand-new life in New Zealand.

———

Six decades later, my mother still clearly remembered their ship steaming up Auckland's Waitematā Harbour on a bright autumn day in 1952. She and Basil were mesmerised by the intense colour of the sky, the sea, the land. Within days of their arrival, my mother – never one to sit back – secured a secretarial job at the bank where my father worked. They lived in a small cottage near the sea on the north shore of Auckland, and each work day they caught a bus and a lumbering ferry across the harbour to the city. They had a sensible plan: save for a house deposit before starting a family.

In what was probably carelessness in a passionate moment, my mother soon became pregnant with me. Basil was dismayed. This unplanned baby was an expensive burden. Perhaps it was then that his private gloom started, but my mother's happiness really began. Finally, she would have a person who belonged to her.

———

Today, no trace remains of the hospital beneath One Tree Hill where I was born. Cornwall Park Hospital had been built about a decade before my birth, as the 39th General US Army Hospital for the casualties expected as the Second World War extended into the Pacific. When the war in the Pacific did not escalate and the Americans left, the New Zealand government kept some of the buildings as a temporary women's hospital.

Inside that hospital in 1953, dozens of women contributed to the post-war baby boom. For my parents, and no doubt for the medical staff attending my difficult birth, I was simply another pale-skinned baby, lucky to be born into this little country whose allies had won the dreadful war. The nurses proclaimed me 'normal and bonny', though I did have a raspberry birthmark – a haemangioma – on my chest, the standard radiation treatment for which seeded a cancer that would disrupt my later life.

My parents gave little thought to how my being born in this place might shape my identity and who I might become. I would have opportunities, they thought, and live in a beautiful landscape in the fresh air, away from the cramped cities of England, the post-war deprivations, and the crushing constraints of a class system. That was enough for them. They did not know that I was born into a doubled space, where things have more than one meaning.

———

So I was born beneath two quite different but identical hills. If infants can be said to see anything, my first glimpse of land was not simply One Tree Hill. That volcanic cone, rising high amongst all the other remnant volcanoes in the

Auckland area, has another name, another history and another
identity.

It is Maungakiekie: mountain of the kiekie vine. The
kiekie vine, with its woody stem and flax-like leaves, used to
entwine the large forest trees that grew on and around the hill.
According to Māori, Kiekie had a brother named Harakeke.
Harakeke, the flax bush, left home to live with Wainui, the
mother of waters, while Kiekie stayed with Tāne, the lord of
the forest, 'piggy-backing on his shoulders wherever he went'.[1]
Where there are no suitable trees to climb, kiekie forms an
impassable tangle on cool, moist ground. The people harvested
its edible fruit, and kiekie's strong leaves made clothing, mats,
belts, baskets, kites and strands for decorative tukutuku
weaving.

For about six hundred years, people had lived around
the region's volcanic cones, and cultivated extensive kūmara
gardens in its richly volcanic soils. Bounded by two harbours
teeming with fish, the area came to be called Tāmaki-makau-rau
or Tāmaki-desired-by-many.[2] The largest volcano, Maungakiekie, with three craters, had been shaped by the Waiohua
people into a huge fortified village or pā with an extensive series
of ridges, paths and food storage pits. The pā was such a vast
feat of earthmoving and construction that, many years after its
wooden buildings and fortifications had disappeared in ruins, a
European historian declared that the craters of Maungakiekie,
'cut into gigantic steps … look not unlike the auditorium of
some noble Colosseum'.[3]

By 1840, it was the Ngāti Whātua people who occupied
the land around the abandoned pā – and Pākehā, largely from
Britain, were seeking territory. In Tāmaki-makau-rau, the Ngāti
Whātua leader Te Kawau shrewdly offered land to the new

colonial government for a capital city, believing that a solid Pākehā presence in the area would protect his people from aggressive northern tribes and enrich them through trade. For Māori, inviting settlement was not a simple act of alienating territory to new owners, it was a complex act of manaaki, a sort of relational generosity to affirm an ongoing relationship with mutual benefits.

The Pākehā officials, with a very different view of land ownership based in British law, sold the land to individual settlers for vast profits, and the low ridges and gentle valleys of what was called Auckland were modified and divided into streets for housing and commerce. A city was established quickly, and European settlers flowed in. Ngāti Whātua, rather than being a part of its planned development on territory they were sharing with the newcomers, found themselves at the margins of the growing city. At the same time, the new settlement was reliant on Māori labour and industry. Pākehā needed the vegetables and fruit grown by Māori on their rich soils, and the timber, flour, flax and other produce from iwi further afield.

By the time I was born, One Tree Hill held only ghostly evidence of the 'noble Colosseum' of the Waiohua. The acres of terrace, rampart, ditch, and all the earthworks of the citadel that once overlooked the whole area were now blurred beneath its European blanket of bright green grass, and a scattering of munching sheep. And at the summit of the pā, in the place of a sacred tōtara tree, chopped down by a careless settler, stood a solitary Monterey pine.

———

So what was the hill in whose shadow I was born? One Tree Hill? Or Maungakiekie? This could be dismissed as merely a semantic question: surely one hill can have two names, either of which would do. In fact, since 2014, it officially has a doubled name, joined by a slash. It is Maungakiekie/One Tree Hill.

The slash marks an ongoing tension: the mountain's identity remains unsettled. It is like the old rabbit–duck illusion. A single image is of a duck *and* a rabbit, but it cannot be both at the same time. A rabbit is not a duck, and vice versa. Likewise, Maungakiekie is not the same as One Tree Hill. A place *is* its stories; without its stories, a place might still vibrate with its own thingly power, but for human beings, its human-made stories are compelling. The stories of Maungakiekie and One Tree Hill, the histories that call those places into being, are quite different.

My parents saw only One Tree Hill that stood in the centre of a park donated to the city by the owner, John Logan Campbell.[4] They could not say what caused its terraced shape, and the name 'Maungakiekie', if they ever heard it, would have been a scramble of foreign sounds. Maungakiekie – and Kiekie, the Waiohua and Ngāti Whātua – were not merely invisible to Basil and Ruth, they simply did not exist. In this my parents were like many of their contemporaries, whether local or immigrant.

I like to imagine that newborns, not yet shaped by either knowledge or ignorance, are naturally open to multiplicity; that I felt the spirits of the land under my crib; that I sensed the lingering gods of the kūmara gardens and Kiekie once riding on Tāne's shoulders in this place. I want to believe I was somehow aware of the souls of those massacred by waves of fighting on the land on which I was born, the defeated Waiohua,

the victorious Ngāti Whātua hapū, the warring Ngāpuhi from
the north, and the rangatira Te Kawau's decision to share the
land with the powerful Pākehā; that I could sense John Logan
Campbell's love of this land, and the spirit or āhua of the
murdered tōtara tree at the summit of the hill.

But my spirit imaginings are more fantasy than memory.
The very English squirrels decorating my crib did not chatter
about Kiekie or his friends; my mother sang me songs about
riding a cock-horse to Banbury Cross, and Humpty Dumpty
falling from a wall. I was oblivious to the ancient metaphysical
forces of the land and its people. However, there I was at the
beginning, taking my first breath and opening my eyes under
the maru – the shelter – of Maungakiekie/One Tree Hill.

My mountain would always morph, in a blur of ghostly
unsettling movement, between One Tree Hill and Maungakiekie. Instead of trying to find a single clear narrative for the
hill, I would feel *both* dynamic histories, always rubbing uncom-
fortably against each other. The necessary doubled vision that
brought to life both Maungakiekie *and* One Tree Hill, or more
crucially, the relationship between them, was a skill I would
learn as I grew into an identity my parents never claimed: that
of Pākehā.

Learning to stand upright

As the _Tamaroa_ steamed up the Waitematā Harbour in April 1952, my young parents arriving in Auckland were oblivious to a disturbing scene unfolding on the nearby shore. Ngāti Whātua were being evicted from the last remnants of their harbourside lands. Their village had been deemed an unsanitary slum and a public eyesore – and unsuitable for the imminent visit of the new Queen Elizabeth. By July that year, bulldozers had torn away Ngāti Whātua's wharenui and kāinga at Ōrākei, and the people had been persuaded – or forced – to relocate into state rental housing on a nearby ridge. Only a tiny graveyard at Ōkahu Bay remained of all their previous lands in the area.[1] The _Auckland Star_ newspaper marked the event with a photograph captioned 'Maori Shacks Go Up in Smoke'.

By the time I was born, the dispossession of local Māori in Auckland was accompanied by a population expansion from elsewhere. Three migrations were swelling Tāmaki-makau-rau. Māori from other tribal regions were moving in. Hundreds of Māori families had begun the greatest migration since their forebears arrived in Aotearoa, moving from rural villages and farms to work on the wharves, in labouring jobs and in the factories of central Auckland. Meanwhile, immigrant workers from the islands of the Pacific were being sought for unskilled and low-paid positions in the post-war economic boom. The other main migrants were the British Europeans

– including Ruth and Basil – making their way into relatively well-paid positions as bankers, shopkeepers, factory owners, schoolteachers, businessmen and government officials.

Māori – as well as the immigrant Pacific people – were by now firmly located at the edges of a Pākehā-dominated Auckland, finding work where they could, with many living in the run-down houses of the inner city west of Queen Street. I was soon to live nearby.

———

When I was ten days old, my parents took me from the hospital to their tiny flat above the Bank of New Zealand's Newton branch in Karangahape Road, where Basil now worked (a flat came with the job). The grand old bank building on the corner of West Street no longer exists; in its place is a bridge over the motorway where rows of dense traffic move north–south across the isthmus.

Through the winter of 1954, my mother pushed me in my comfortable English pram along Karangahape Road to the park next to the cemetery where the early Pākehā city fathers were buried, or through St Kevin's Arcade down to Myers Park. We did not venture into the shabby but lively suburbs nearby – Freemans Bay and Ponsonby – where the Māori and Pacific families lived. My mother had heard the stories of poverty and violence, of families having their power cut off by the authorities, of kids going without adequate food or clothing. I meanwhile was learning to walk in the button-up blue leather and cardboard-soled shoes sent from England. I still have those shoes, scuffed and desiccated artefacts from another world.

At the time that I was literally learning 'the trick of standing upright', Karangahape Road on the ridge above the two harbours was a lively Auckland shopping destination, busy and crowded. It was one of the few streets in Auckland city with a Māori name, and Ruth took to calling it 'The Road' to avoid having to wrap her English tongue around the strange, long word. There was even public (Pākehā) discussion about replacing Karangahape with an English name. These days it is almost universally known as 'K Road'.

In taking my first steps on that street, I was following an old Māori walking route between the two harbours, the Waitematā and the Manukau. A number of stories explain its name. One says that Hape, a Tainui ancestor who arrived in Aotearoa on a giant stingray, came to the Manukau Harbour and, marking the boundaries of his territory there, shouted his presence to Tāne Mahuta, the god of the forest. 'Te Karanga a Hape' refers to 'the calling out by Hape'.[2]

On these excursions, my mother and I encountered Māori children going to and from nearby schools. With mild disapproval, my mother recalls that Māori people 'never seemed to walk around on their own, particularly the school-children, who were always laughing and playing.' They were, she remembers, 'always in bare feet and you could hear them before you could see them'.

In later years, I asked my mother whether she knew any Māori people in Auckland then. She answered, after a pause, defensively. 'I wanted to, but it wasn't possible in those days. They didn't mix. The two races just naturally didn't mix. Like sheep and horses in a paddock, we each kept to our own kind,' she told me. I did not ask how she knew what Māori naturally wanted.

My parents had joined the population of European New Zealanders confused about their relationship with Māori. In the cities and larger towns, many Europeans did not know any Māori unless they worked together. They believed that Māori people were generally happy and that there was little active discrimination against them. But their complacency was tinged with a persistent anxiety.

This feeling was expressed in a frank editorial in the *Auckland Star*, a few days before I was born, on 12 September 1953. The piece began:

> For sixty years and more public speakers have asserted that New Zealand has no major 'native trouble.' ... The modern version of this way of thinking aloud is that there is neither Pakeha nor Maori, in that all are New Zealanders, and all have equal rights under the law. There is not, nor will there be, any discrimination.

But, the editorial continued, such assertions about sameness and equality make it 'only the more difficult to put into precise words some of the thoughts which are beginning to trouble us'. In truth, there is 'unmistakably, a growing fear – a fear extremely difficult to state in words – that all is not as well as it might be'. The writer hastened to add that 'there is not, at the moment, a major problem in relationships [but] there is at least a suspicion that those things which are going amiss now that the Maori has "come to town" in numbers, may be hardening into a major problem'.

The piece does not identify those things 'going amiss' in the towns, but it seems fair to assume that it was referring to Māori poverty, unemployment and homelessness, as well as to Pākehā racism, known in those days as 'discrimination'. Speaking on behalf of what he considers to be the majority of his readers, the editor says that it is tempting to take refuge in indifference: 'Let the Maori look after himself. After all, we've done a lot for him, haven't we?'

But, the editor goes on, 'even as we say something like that, there is the uneasy thought that such an attitude won't do anything but hasten the day when it may be impossible to conceal the existence of a genuine "Maori problem".'[3]

What did he mean, I wonder, by a 'Māori problem'? Did he discern Māori anger and resentment at the loss of their land, their economic base, and their social structures attributable to the Pākehā? Or was there perhaps a suggestion of a Pākehā problem with Māori – a Pākehā inability to understand or engage with Māori, expressed by my mother as 'they don't mix'?

———

My mother remembers sitting with me on a park bench near Karangahape Road, when 'a stout Māori woman, with a bright green scarf' sat down and struck up a conversation, admiring the baby and asking Ruth: 'Where do you stay?' The phrase distinguishes between the place a person lives and the tribal region they identify as 'home' – and my mother was momentarily confused. But she responded warmly, and they had 'a nice conversation'. The woman's name was Clarissa, which Ruth remembers 'because it was so English, not a Māori name'.

My mother, wanting new friends, was feeling her way into her new country. She had a natural English politeness that eschewed being too friendly or 'nosy'. This manner had been officially noted as contrasting with an apparent Māori tendency towards friendliness. *Meet New Zealand*, a 1942 booklet

produced for US servicemen stationed in New Zealand, pointed
to this reserve among Pākehā, comparing it with the relative
openness of Māori: on the one hand, 'the Maori retains those
old habits of generosity, friendliness, hospitality, helpfulness in
times of trouble that the white man has almost forgotten'. And
on the other, 'As a people we [Pākehā] are rather reserved and
undemonstrative, may even seem cold and unfriendly [but] …
our hearts are reasonably big.'[4] These days, New Zealanders
are known worldwide as friendly people; the reserve of English
immigrants is now seen as an old-fashioned quality, diminished
over the years by Pākehā proximity to Māori warmth. For Māori,
however, the reserve is still noticed as a 'Pākehā thing'.

Packed within this observation of English reserve, it seems
to me, is the nub of the Pākehā 'native problem', even to this
day. To be reserved is to be slightly distant from others, to be
cautious about familiar engagement especially with strangers.
Yet warmth and generosity are qualities (known as manaaki)
that Māori hold dear, so it is not hard to imagine that they
often find Pākehā difficult to relate to. But manaaki is not just
about being nice. It requires an engagement; it is an invitation
to a relationship; it exists in an *exchange*. Pākehā often miss
this in their admiration of Māori friendliness: something is
required of us.

Chatting in the sun on Karangahape Road in 1954, my
mother and Clarissa were on two sides of a divide created by
European inability to engage in an exchange that required us to
be open to, or even curious about, a Māori point of view. Ruth
could not imagine the alienation, poverty and gross humiliation
that her people, the Pākehā settlers, soldiers, lawmakers and
government officials, had inflicted on Clarissa's people. We
had acquired their land and their livelihoods and now, when we

wanted to acquire them as friends, they seemed (despite the friendliness of women like Clarissa), as Ruth put it, to 'keep to themselves'. Our reserve was projected onto them as a fault.

This perverse sense that Pākehā have of being rejected by a people they have so systematically alienated seems to me now to be a none-too-complicated strategy to insulate Pākehā from our uneasiness about the past, an uneasiness we feel whether we know details of that past or not. We find the relationship with Māori difficult and we look for someone to blame for causing our difficulties. To feel rejected is a subtle way of shifting blame for our 'problems with Māori' to Māori themselves.

The rejection my English mother experienced most keenly came from Pākehā. 'Māori people never criticised me,' she told me later, 'but plenty of Europeans did. I was always being called a Pom, as a negative, and Pākehās made it clear they did not like the influx of Pommie immigrants who were "taking our jobs".' Public scorn was aimed at her large English pram, in which I sat, cheerfully oblivious: 'You might need that in your cold and foggy Pommie weather, missus, but not here!'

She remembers parking the pram at the bottom of the stairs, and carrying me up to our small flat above the bank, in tears about this lack of welcome by the European New Zealanders.

———

I was just getting the hang of walking when my mother became pregnant again, and I was taken from the lovely Tāmaki-makau-rau. My father, seeking a geographical solution to his haunting depression, had a new job in the South Island. He was to be treasurer for the borough council in Blenheim, in Marlborough, on the drained swamp lands of the Wairau River.

In Blenheim, by the end of June 1955, twins had been born: a boisterous boy and a fussy, crying girl. I was twenty-one months old, and became my mother's lieutenant, carrying clean nappies, rocking my sister's crib, or propping up a bottle for my hungry brother. I was a sensitive and busy child, keen to help. I did have my own life as well. I kept a little suitcase containing some buttons, a silky scarf, and a book. My mother told me about these things; I cannot remember them.

I do not recall ghosts in Blenheim, though the area must have been thick with them. The first armed conflict of the New Zealand Wars took place nearby. The ink was barely dry on the 1840 Treaty of Waitangi that protected Māori rights to their own lands when, in June 1843, armed settlers from Nelson illegally attempted to take the Wairau Valley, where Māori from different hapū had for generations irrigated rich soils for extensive gardens. In resistance, the rangatira Te Rauparaha and Te Rangihaeata and their Ngāti Toa kinsmen who occupied the area at the time had chased off the surveyors, removed equipment, and burnt their reed huts. In the ensuing conflict, twenty-two Europeans and four Māori were killed, including the chiefs' wives. Te Rauparaha was clear that the Pākehā greed for land was the foundation of all the troubles: 'The Europeans say it is theirs,' he told the Governor, 'but who says so besides themselves. ... We heard of the sale [but] we never agreed to that sale, and we never received any payment.'[5]

Because the Pākehā actions had been illegal, Robert FitzRoy, the Governor of the time, announced there would be no official retaliation for the European deaths, some of which were executions following surrender. There was outrage from

the settlers. Pākehā persisted in the area, and in 1855 a soggy
settlement of riverside tents and shacks on the swampy flood
plains called Waiharakeke (flax swamp) by Māori was named
'Beaver Town', and later Blenheim after the Battle of Blenheim
in Germany, in which the English were victorious in 1704.

I barely remember the place. We lived in a rented upstairs
flat in the grand Waterlea House, the old homestead of a former
Pākehā landowner, since demolished. Only a few glimpses
survive from my infant memory: a black-and-white cat vomiting
on the landing; deep clean water running through oxygen
weed in a stream near the house; new toys from England on a
polished floor; and handkerchiefs pegged on my own washing
line hung between two garden trees. One day I fell down the
stairs, according to my mother, and broke my leg, but I have no
memory of that.

It was only two years before my tense father – who never
understood babies, and who no doubt felt trapped – moved us
again, this time back to the North Island, and a promotion to
head accountant for the Dannevirke Hospital. I was four years
old. It was not to be a happy move.

Finding boundaries

It was dark in Dannevirke. The heaviness of the light, so far from the ocean and the close, glowering Ruahine Range, pulled the whole world into a low suffocating space between earth and sky. In this thick space I made my first Māori friend – or thought I did.

We must have arrived in Dannevirke in the winter, because our house was so cold. It was colder than anything I had experienced. I dreaded bedtime; it took courage to crawl between the sheets on the freezing kapok mattress and the inadequate woollen blankets. 'Ride your bike! Ride your bike!' called my mother, encouraging me to pump my little legs up and down to generate enough friction to get warm.

Strange scenes are vivid in my memory, way before I started school: barking dogs trying to bite the tyres of our first car, a little Austin, as we drove along rural roads; a six-legged lamb born in the paddock next door; a boy with scarred hands burned by a bull's saliva (so he told me); my father shooting a possum from a lamp post, as its doomed baby clung to its fur; my brother tasting toxic liquid from an old bottle found in the weeds behind the shed and having to be rushed to the hospital. I spent my first months in this gothic place in a trance of morbid discovery.

My twin siblings, Gillian and Richard, were now toddlers, and my responsibilities increased. I had to double-check that they kept on their woollen hats and coats when we were outside, and I helped them on and off the hard wood-and-iron swings at the Domain. I anxiously watched my impulsive brother in case he ran out on the road.

I felt lonely at home. I have no visceral memory of being held close to the body of my mother, no sense of love or real warmth, no recollection of family laughter. My mother, preoccupied with two babies and an unhappy husband, with no wider family support, and burdened by her own lack of maternal love, spread thin her small supply of affection. In a photograph, I clutch a hard-bodied doll. I am looking up at the camera with a forced and anxious smile. Perhaps I am worried about what the photographer expects of me.

My happiest moments were spent reading books with my mother. Parcels from the place she called 'Home' would arrive at Christmas and on birthdays. My father's mother sent children's books and, later, English comics *Princess* and *Buster*. I quickly learned to read. My mother and her friends expressed open admiration for my reading talents: 'What a clever girl!' 'She'll go far!' They clapped with delight. Here was the affection and regard I wanted. I became hungrily addicted to praise for 'being smart'.

Naturally, for a clever but lonely girl who craved love and attention, kindergarten was a haven. The teachers warmed to me because I could write and read, and I had developed precocious organising skills at home so I tidied up toys and paints. I had found my element: the classroom. By the time I was four years old, I had a sense that my emotional safe place would be in my mind, in knowing things, and through school achievement. I know now that I was wrong about setting my sights on school success as an 'emotional safe place'. As an

adult, I found that my pursuit of such success required a debil-
itating reliance on others' attention and approval. My lauded
achievements did not bring me the joy I had hoped they would.
A split had formed within me between what others thought I
should be like and what I secretly felt.

This dual life – the achieving-girl outside, the feeling-girl
inside – may have been painful for many years, but ultimately it
became richly productive as I drew myself together. Although
I could never have guessed it then, it was my relationships with
Māori that would bring my own two selves together, at the same
time as opening up the idea of 'two worlds'.

———

My mother became pregnant again. She sought an abortion
(she told me later), but her doctor, Dr Hunter, had simply glared
at her: 'You have three beautiful children, and there is no reason
why you should not have more,' he said. She ended up having
two more.

We moved into another bitterly cold wooden house, this
time in the middle of a paddock on Hospital Street, across the
road from my father's office at the hospital. The uneven floors
were covered with thin linoleum, and my industrious mother
covered the walls with patterned wallpaper to cheer the place
up. She sewed quilts for our beds, and warm children's coats
and sturdy new shoes arrived from England. My father built
a chook house and bought a flock of brown hens and brightly
coloured bantams. He also set up beehives on a friend's
paddock, and a honey-house in the backyard where he could
extract the honey he collected.

As I grew older, my mother allowed me to roam over the

nearby countryside or ride away on my bicycle with friends for a whole day. She believed in busy, adventurous children. So my friends, siblings and I would watch birds, climb trees, fire pebbles at targets from our shanghais, make fires and roast huhu grubs or boil freshwater crayfish or cook damper bread, get muddy in the nearby swamps, and get spooked at the local cemetery. We would chase headless chickens, their necks dripping blood, from the chopping block down to the swamp. I would hide my face when my neighbour caught one of the sheep that grazed in the paddock, its legs helplessly pawing the air while he slit its throat. I liked the scent of the moist grass in its glistening guts as they spilled out on the ground.

I loved and feared that landscape in equal measure. I loved the smells of the damp, muddy earth, the sharp fresh air, the warm, steaming cowpats, the wet wool of the sheep. I loved the trunks and stout reliable branches of pine and macrocarpa. I loved the magpies' harsh calls, and the beauty of the scratchy wētā. These became part of my being.

But the magpies also terrified me when they swooped and pecked; the toetoe leaves sliced and bloodied my bare legs; mournful paddocks, terraced by sheep tracks and scored by drains, were littered with grass-covered rotting logs, revealing the sad remains of forest; the dark remaining bush seemed strange, hostile, ghost-filled.

Above it all, the dark indigo Ruahine mountains were perpetually threatening. We never went into them except to pass through the Manawatū Gorge in our car on our way to Palmerston North. I sat nervously on the back seat of our lumbering 1939 Plymouth, always only inches away from plunging down the side of the ravine and into the Manawatū River.

My parents may have been grieving for England. I do not know. Aside from marvelling at the bright colours of their adopted country, and rejoicing in their children's freedom, they never expressed any real pleasure in the wild places beyond the local district. My father was intent on domesticating the land – growing a garden with rows of vegetables, planting fruit trees, stacking cut wood and putting up sturdy fences. Every week my busy but dutiful mother found time to write 'Home' to Basil's mother on tissue-thin blue aerogramme paper with long, newsy accounts of family life, and each week a letter came back. My mother forced me to write to our grandmother, but I never knew what to tell someone I did not know. During this period, I was surprised one afternoon to find my mother sobbing at her sewing machine; the woman who owned the orphanage in Essex where my mother grew up had died. I knew my mother disliked that woman, and I wondered why she was so upset.

It somehow felt as though we were marooned, though I was too young to know what we were separated from. All I knew was that *I was here* in this wonderful, absorbing and frightening place.

———

School would change everything. Here I discovered some-thing quite new: categories of people aside from 'adults' and 'children'. I felt myself bursting with questions as I encountered 'Catholics' and 'Chinese' and 'Māori' people.

I came to know about Catholics when, at five, I was allowed to walk the mile to school with my neighbours. Near my school, waiting on the pavement each morning for their bus, was a quiet cluster of kids in brown school uniforms. 'Catholics!' hissed a little friend as we passed the silent crowd. My friend taught me a sing-song chant, which we would sing from a safe distance: 'Catholic dogs, sitting on logs, eat-ing bell-ies out of frogs.' My question at home, 'what is a Catholic?', elicited my father's scorn. 'They believe in some gobbledygook,' was all he seemed capable of explaining. 'And they send their children to a special school to learn it.' I was mystified by my friend's chant, and my father's answer, but learned that lines were to be drawn: some children were like 'us' and some were not.

My introduction to Chinese people was similar, in some ways. I had seen only one Chinese person. He sold fresh vegetables off the back of his horse-drawn cart, whose iron-shod wheels crunched on the road. I knew him as Joe, though I found out later he was Chung Lee. He and his family had a market garden on the edge of town. He seemed kind, but as mysterious as the bottom of the ocean.

I learned most about the Chinese from a book. A favourite amongst my picture books was *The Story About Ping*, by the American writer Marjorie Flack. I adored the book's illustra-tions, and fell in love with Ping. I can still recall the opening lines: 'Once upon a time there was a beautiful young duck named Ping. Ping lived with his mother and his father and two sisters and three brothers and eleven aunts and seven uncles and forty-two cousins. Their home was a boat with two wise eyes on the Yangtze River.' What a wonderful new sound 'Yangtze' was. And what could be more romantic than living on a boat with all those relatives?

But the cruel story disturbed me. Ping walked each day in a line with his large family to feed in the river. In the evening, he was always very careful not to be late home, because the last duck always got a spanking from the ducks' owner. One evening, when he found himself last, Ping hid. Next day, he was all alone on the river and a small boy caught him. 'I will cook him with rice at sunset tonight,' said the boy's mother. The boy released Ping, who quickly paddled back to his wise-eyed boat as night fell. SPANK went the cane on Ping's back, but he was happy, home with his cousins.

Perhaps because I had no cousins to share a warm nest with, I was drawn again and again to the story. I stared often at the yellow-coloured people in the illustrations, worrying about their cruelty to the ducks they hit or cooked and wondering at their appearance. I liked their almond-shaped eyes, and would stretch the sides of my eyes each time I passed the bathroom mirror, admiring the effect.

One weekend, I made a shocking discovery. I was sitting with some neighbour children on a grassy bank next to the hospital parking area, chanting a favourite ditty: 'Ching Chong Chinaman went to milk a cow; Ching Chong Chinaman didn't know how. Ching Chong Chinaman pulled the wrong tit, and all he got was a bucket of ...' The last, unspeakably naughty word was replaced with a nervous laugh, every time. A pleasant-looking Pākehā man, walking to his car, approached us intrepid balladeers: 'You must not sing that song,' he said firmly. 'It is not nice to Chinese people.' Never having been reprimanded by a stranger before, I was mortified, and I took the lesson to heart. We never sang the song again, and I began to wonder why some people were not liked. Was it because of their eyes? Their cruelty to animals? In the case of Catholics, could it be the colour of their school uniforms?

———

I decided not to ask my father any of these questions. I sensed that his answers would not satisfy me. He was happy to scorn Catholics; I worried that he would ridicule the Chinese. I knew that my father disliked 'Japs' and Germans, too, the cunning, evil enemies from the war, their angry faces familiar to me from my brothers' English comics. I had to presume he was right about them, but alarming cracks were appearing in the world: my father could be wrong. This knowledge only intensified my secret inner world's ghostly half-ideas and an inchoate sense of curiosity that felt dangerously daring.

And then there were Māori. At school we learned Māori stories – myths and legends, as they were called – such as the stories of the hero Māui, who slowed the sun with his thick ropes to make the working day longer. I was somehow aware that some of the children in the school were Māori because of their skin colour, though I was pretty hazy about the relationship between them and Māui. We learned Māori stick games which we played with rolled-up newspapers, and enthusiastically mimicked the delicious sounds of songs with unknown meanings: 'Me he manu rere ahau e / kua rere ki tō moenga / ki te awhi tō tinana / auē, auē / e te tau, tahuri mai'. (If I were a bird on the wing / I would fly to your bed / to embrace your body / Oh! Oh! / My darling, turn to me.)

But, mostly, I was aware of the term 'Māori' only as a negative adjective. I knew the phrase 'Māori land' because my father had uttered it disapprovingly when we went out in our Plymouth on a Sunday drive in the country. He applied it to land that was understocked and undeveloped, its fences broken or its hillsides taken over by vigorous European weeds such as gorse, ragwort and thistle. I remember kneeling up on the brown leather car seat, staring out at the 'Māori land', curious about my father's derision, and sad for land that had no one to care for it.

As well as 'Māori land', my father spoke of 'Māori houses' (always run-down), and there were 'Māori colours' (garish), 'Māori time' (late), 'Māori dogs' (cunning), and 'Māori cars' (broken or dented). The most mysterious category was the 'Māori pā'. I had learned at school that a pā was a fortified hill village in the olden days. Admonishing me for adding 'ay?' at the end of a sentence, my mother would growl, 'You sound like you've been dragged up in a Māori par.' The children at school spoke a form of Pākehā English that followed a Māori speech pattern, replacing the more traditional 'ne?' with 'ay?' to solicit agreement. The idea of being dragged up in a Māori pā conjured up a sense of being pulled along on dusty ground, near rough fortifications, in a distant place. The prospect, far from being awful, was vaguely intriguing.

Relatively few Māori children attended the North School – most lived in surrounding rural areas, such as Tahoraiti (which we pronounced 'Ta-ridy') and Kaitoke ('Kai-toe-key'), and caught a bus to South School. But I liked the brown kids who were at my school: Hemi with his name knitted into the pattern of his jersey; Tom the handsome flirt with adult-style slicked-back hair; and the many kids of the energetic Hana family.

The Hanas lived on my walking route to school. There was always activity at their house, always someone outside sitting on the boards of the front verandah, and a scattering of objects around the garden. Hana men seemed constantly to be fixing engines, their heads under the bonnet of a car in the driveway. Most interesting to me was a brown stain on the house, where Mrs Hana emptied her teapot out of the kitchen window. Equally shocking was the sight of the smallest Hana girls hanging upside down on the school jungle gym with no knickers on, shrieking with laughter. Their siblings and cousins thought this was a huge joke.

These acts of reckless disregard for decency thrilled me. People were getting on with life, amusing each other, not worrying about external appearances, and I was secretly delighted. I was now seven or eight years old, and the boundaries of my 'real' world – as opposed to the universe created by my parents and my books – seemed to be expanding. Other possibilities, other worlds, were becoming visible at the edges of my own.

There are two Māori girls I particularly remember: Linda, a beautiful girl who had the shiniest black silk hair I had ever seen, and Maria, who had a wide smile and laughed a lot. Linda was painfully shy; she tended to play small games with the quiet girls. Maria was confident and outgoing; she ran everywhere, and everyone, including me, wanted to be her friend. She barely noticed me, but once, as we sat on the benches along the sunny back wall of the school, I shared my lunchtime sandwiches with her. I felt happy just to be in her company. Beside her, I felt somehow braver, bigger, more daring. Her world seemed large and happy, full of friends and relations; my own felt anxious and small by comparison.

Both Maria and Linda lived in Robert Street, a state-housing area over the road from the school. There was always something going on in that street. One day, after school, I heard a scream. One of the boys had thrown a wooden clothes peg, in which a sharpened nail had been fixed, at a girl riding her bike. The nail embedded itself in her calf, and she fell off her bike, shrieking as though she was dying. The boys fled. Horrified, I watched blood trickle down the girl's leg as one of the older girls snatched the nail out. Kids crowded around the howling child as she hobbled into the nearby house, and I wondered if the boys would get a hiding.

I did not tell my parents about any of these things. I somehow knew that they would disapprove; I found I had secrets.

One day, Maria invited me to her place for lunch. I remember this vividly. It was forbidden for pupils to go outside the school gate without permission, but Maria disregarded such details. We crossed the road, and I ran after her, clutching my lunchbox. I remember fishing gear near the house, buoys, tumbled rope nets and buckets. The door was open and I followed Maria inside.

The air in the house was warm and moist, with a strong smell of meat cooking. In the small kitchen were Maria's mother, father and an uncle, all sitting around a table. I was apprehensive. My own mother was always unhappy about people arriving uninvited at meal times, but Maria's mother was relaxed. And she talked and laughed easily with her daughter, as if they were friends. On the table was an enormous pot from which Maria's Dad was serving steaming liquid called a 'boil-up'. When he asked me if I wanted any, I said politely 'no, thank you'.

Maria showed me her bedroom. It was designed for two single beds, but there were three jammed in, for her and her two sisters. Each was covered in a yellow candlewick bedspread. There was no space to walk round the beds, and we crawled across them. As we lay on the beds, I marvelled, in my own childlike way, at how different this life was. Maria and her friends broke all the rules: they ran across the road, they did not bring a lunchbox to school, they shouted and laughed, they had crowded bedrooms, the children were allowed opinions. It was possible to be happy even though you broke the rules. This was a revelation, and I held on to it like a precious treasure.

———

In my house, there were rules, 'The Jones Rules'. My mother, like my father, had her ideas about social propriety, and held a clear distinction between what was acceptable and what was 'common'. The Jones Rules were not written anywhere, but our mother let us know when we broke them: they had to do with correct clothing, tidy hair, good manners and behaviour, 'keeping good company', and observing good grammar and pronunciation. We were not to stay inside on a sunny day, and we could never admit to being bored. We were not to read stories by Enid Blyton (poor literature) or Disney comics (not literature), and it was necessary 'always to have a good book to read'.

Adding to the books we received from England for birthdays and Christmas, every Friday night we would stock up on books from the town library, a large brick building near the main shops. We had a weekly limit of five books each. My favourite was *Anne of Green Gables* by L.M. Montgomery, a Canadian story about a plucky orphan girl. I imagined myself to be Anne: independent, misunderstood, heroic and an orphan. I remember only two New Zealand books: *Richard-Bird in the Bush*, by Molly Miller Atkinson, about a town sparrow visiting the native birds of the New Zealand bush; and A.W. Reed's *Wonder Tales of Maoriland* about Māui's many adventures.

Because it was required reading for a Brownies book badge, I skim-read Stella Morice's *The Book of Wiremu*, about a Māori boy's life beside a river, but it contained too many unfamiliar

Māori words. The New Zealand books about, say, Māui or
Wiremu had a certain teacherly tone that I resisted – I wanted
excitement rather than worthy adventure – and the Māori
characters seemed nothing like the kids at school. The other
thing that put me off local stories was that the usual heroes
– whether Māui, Wiremu or Richard-Bird – were boys. I liked
stories about girls.

A book that had a lasting impact was *Presenting Other
People's Children* by Scottish Fabian writer Naomi Mitchison – a
collection of photographs of children from different countries
with text introducing the reader to their varied lives. The
emotional weight of each photograph demanded attention,
and I imagined the life of each child: the thin little girl in Africa,
nearly naked, carrying a pumpkin on her head; the chubby
'Eskimo' squinting from under her fur hood; the blond boy
eating two ice creams in an American fairground. On the final
page was a poem I learned by heart:

> ... there shall be neither rich nor poor,
> Nor privilege nor power,
> But all shall meet in amity
> At the striking of the hour.
> In amity ... in amity ... goodbye till then.[1]

I had no idea what 'amity' meant. I did not want to ask
anyone lest an explanation break the poem's spell. The words
held big ideas about things beyond my proper understanding, things I could only observe and wonder at: rich and poor,
privilege and power. I eventually looked up 'amity' in my pocket
dictionary (another present from England). The idea that
friendship might be at the heart of things made me love the
poem even more.

Each Friday evening after visiting the library, our family would spend time in what we called 'walking up and down the shops', which was a common habit in 1960s New Zealand. All the shops would be open, their lights blazing, and the footpaths under the verandahs along the main street would be crowded with people in their good clothes, walking and stopping to chat with friends. Shops were not open on the weekends in those days. Thanks to government subsidies and a strong export market, the sheep farmers were well-off then, and the Pākehā and Māori farmers and farm workers and their families would come to town for a Friday treat.

On Friday nights I kept an eye out for the children from school. When one of them shouted 'Hey, Alison!' I would wave, pleased to be noticed, hoping my parents saw that I had friends – and a life – they did not know about. One evening, a Māori girl stopped. She thrust forward a damp steaming newspaper parcel ripped open at the top and asked, 'Hey, wanna chip?'. I quickly put a salty, soggy potato chip in my mouth, breathing quickly to cool my tongue. I knew I would be in trouble. 'Don't take food from other people' was a Jones Rule. So was not eating in public, especially not from a ripped fish-and-chip parcel, and certainly not with your mouth open. Nevertheless, a powerful attraction to my Māori friends' devil-may-care attitudes trumped my mother's disapproval; their cheerfulness secretly buoyed me.

The Māori kids broke plenty of other Jones Rules. Some of the older girls wore patent-leather shoes and belts, which my mother, for some reason, considered the height of bad taste. Wearing jandals and jeans were a sign of being 'common', too, not to mention going barefoot in town on a Friday night. Some of the men even held their trousers up with twine. Then there was the loud laughing and shouting, and the quirky expression 'hey e-haw!' (e-haw was a form of 'e hoa', friend). Such language was not only vulgar, but a lower-class European bad habit as well, and the Joneses were 'better than that'.

There is another strong memory of my developing inner critic from this time. When my youngest brother Garrick was born, Dad began buying a weekly Golden Kiwi lottery ticket. He wrote 'Seven Up' on the ticket, referring to the five children and two adults in the family as well as the name of a popular fizzy drink. Dad used to pin the thin yellow paper ticket to the butcher's calendar next to the kitchen stove. The 1962 calendar displayed a pretty white house with red roses by a front door, a closely cut lawn and a confident, slightly aloof air. Mum said that if we won the Golden Kiwi, we would buy a house like that. I often stared at the picture, but the house did not enchant me. I did not want a neat, solid little cottage, but something wilder: a tree hut perhaps, something quirkier ... more defiant.

In rejecting my parents' aspirations, and dreaming of elsewhere, I may have been influenced by the rebellious mood of the new decade. Social change made more interesting the news reports on the radio, to which my parents listened every morning and evening. African countries were seeking independence from the British empire, and civil rights struggles by Black activists in the United States were getting global attention. The charismatic John F. Kennedy was in power. I still recall the tears and shock on the morning we awoke to the news that he had been assassinated. The neighbouring kids' mother, Mrs Eccles-Smith, bought Beatles records, which we loved as we crowded around her little portable record player on their living-room carpet. They sang 'Please Please Me', and someone gave me a plastic Beatles wig and an orange Beatles poster. I was in love with Paul McCartney, and the world was changing.

———

In the meantime, that visit to Maria's family had set off something within me, resetting my personal compass. Those small glimpses of a different kind of life had awakened a deep yearning for something richer and warmer that lay beyond the boundaries of my own experience. I was learning about the limits of my world. I felt its edges, too, when I looked up at the night sky. I loved to go outside by myself in the evening, into the cold dark, under the towering sky bright with galaxies that went on for ever. Their mystery enchanted me, and I was overwhelmed by a sense of longing for something else, something greater than myself. At the same time, I revelled in not-knowing, in surrendering to being a part of something I could not understand. Its unknowability I found deeply comforting.

But then, in December 1964, we moved again. My parents packed us five children in the back seat of the Plymouth and we headed north, towards the sun. I had just turned eleven. On the day we left, Mrs Eccles-Smith hung a large Union Jack between two upstairs windows. Remembering this now, I suppose the flag gave voice to an uncertain insistence that being British had to mean *something* in this country. Back then, the familiar red-white-and-blue pattern of the Union Jack seemed so strangely out of place that I was aware of my parents' foreignness. I asked my mother why the flag was hanging on the house. 'You'll understand when you're older,' she replied, through tears that I assumed were of sadness at leaving her Dannevirke friends. She would later tell me that she did not want to move again; she was worried about my unhappy father's belief that a new job and a new town would improve his ever-darkening moods.

We were headed to Whakatāne, a place with a wonderful name, by the sea.

Tricky memories

It would be more than fifty years before I saw Maria again. She was still living in Dannevirke. I was settled in Auckland.

I had not been back since my family left for Whakatāne in 1964. I had been lugging a Dannevirke-sized chip on my shoulder from place to place since childhood; it was, I had decided in my adolescence, a limited place from which I had been lucky to escape. For me, Dannevirke was the quintessence of small-town New Zealand: slow, empty and boring. It was a convenient focus for my resentment about missing out on a stimulating city childhood, and it embodied what I imagined were my parents' narrow aspirations and social conservatism. On the other hand, I had loved the freedom of being a child in a small rural town, the warm musty smells of the cows in the paddock by the house, and the magpies' wardle-doodling cries.

I decided to return to Dannevirke for a few days. I would visit Maria, and recall my first interactions with a Māori family.

———

It was a frosty, sunny day when I drove from Palmerston North airport to Dannevirke in my rental car. Maria and I had arranged to meet at a café in the main street. She was hard to miss, unmistakable in staunch sunglasses, colourful scarf and the same confident manner. We hugged warmly. We ordered lunch. After some small talk, I recalled my happy memories of Maria's house and her bedroom. She listened quietly, then she laughed, delighted and bemused.

She did not live on the corner of Robert Street, she says, but two houses down on the other side. She never ran willy-nilly over the main road. She had no sisters. Her bedroom had only one bed. Her father was not a fisherman, but a shearer and fencer. They never put a pot in the middle of the table, but served their boil-up in individual bowls. She couldn't remember me coming for lunch.

With a mild sense of panic, I stared at Maria. 'You are thinking about the Stewarts,' she said. 'A Pākehā family. Their father was a fisherman and they lived on the corner. Josephine Stewart had two sisters.'

For all my adult life, I had traced my interest in the Māori world back to Maria's house on the corner of Robert Street, to her parents' kitchen and her crowded yellow candlewick-covered beds. But it was a Pākehā girl's bedroom and kitchen, not Maria's. I had invented a memory, a pastiche of recollections and obscure feelings. The story of my Māori friend turned out to be a fantasy of the imagined domestic spaces of a Māori family.

I had to accept what she said. Did she remember me *at all*? 'Yes, but only slightly.' She recalls that she did not choose me for her sports team. She apologised, sincerely, for this fifty-six-year-old slight. I laughed, 'Never mind. I was crap at sports!' and she seemed genuinely relieved. And: 'I can remember you reading to us in standard three. You were confident, and very clear and precise. You sat on a chair at the front of the class. When the teacher said "That's as far as we will go today," you would close the book, all prim and proper, and fold your hands on the cover waiting to be told to go back to your seat. All we wanted was to go and play.' I have no memory of this; and I feel a little wounded by that exclusive 'we'.

Maria's account stirs an uneasy memory: being taken by the hand from my primer classroom, walking along the cold corridor with high windows, being lifted up on to a wooden stool, and asked to spell words, in front of a standard class. The teacher's thick leather strap hung beside the blackboard on a nail. 'Look,' sneered the teacher at her students, humiliation her teaching method, 'a primer girl can do it. Why can't you?'

I felt suddenly uncomfortable on my café chair. 'Was I an unbearable smarty-pants, Maria? Did you resent me?' 'No,' she replied, 'because you weren't snobbish with it. And you read really well, with the right tone of voice and everything.' She had graciously let me off the hook. Again, I felt that flash of warmth, a feeling of acceptance. Maria recalled our class doing Highland dancing in our socks. We affectionately remembered our coloured swap beads nestled on cotton wool linings in taped-together matchboxes. With our friends, we skipped doubled thick ropes, jumped on taut elastic, tossed knucklebones, and played marbles, padder tennis and stick games, depending on the season. I was relieved to find some shared memories.

Maria was bright. 'I went right through and got University Entrance. The teachers seemed surprised when I got UE. All the other Māori kids had left school by then. I never tried really, and all my reports said: "Could do better. Needs to concentrate." I was too busy having a good time!' There was her familiar smile again, now tinged with what looked like regret. She added that her parents put emphasis on school achievement, and her father made her read the newspaper out loud every evening after dinner to practise her reading and improve her vocabulary.

Then: 'My mother always made sure my brother and I were clean. "It doesn't cost much for soap and water!" was her saying. A lot of people looked down on us and thought Māori were dirty, so Mum tried to prove that we were just as good. Only now when I look back on it I can see it must have been hard for Mum to stay on top of it.' I recalled the white handkerchief that Linda's mother made her wear like a badge.

Then Maria says something else that saddens me: 'That's one thing I would change. I wish a teacher had told me that I could go to university. No one ever did.' I can't help silently comparing my own educational trajectory with hers. The small privileges of being a Pākehā child had begun to build up for me in Dannevirke. Both our families valued schoolwork, but school was an extension of my home in a way it was not for Maria. The classroom with its order and constraint was a rewarding place for me, the teachers looked and sounded like me, I wanted to be like them, and they praised and nurtured me. That was not Maria's experience, despite her being smart and outgoing.

None of this talk was easy. I had taken Maria onto territory she did not readily enter; I felt uneasily like an exploitative researcher, mining other people's discomfort for my own benefit. But neither of us pulled back from the conversation.

I decided to ask Maria about her experience of racism as a child. She paused, then said: 'When I went to some kid's place to play after school, you could just feel that some parents did not like you because you were Māori, or poor. They did not give you food, and you just played and went home. They didn't offer you a ride or anything.' It hurt, she said, and you could lose your confidence if it happened too often, but 'you just learned to back off'. I had never invited Maria to play at my place. Was it that I thought my mother might not be relaxed about a Māori girl visiting? I can't put my finger on it, but I know that any invitation to Maria would have been something 'special' in our house.

The café owners were stacking the chairs for closing time, and we had both had enough for the day, so we agreed to meet again the next afternoon.

———

Back at my hotel that evening, I recognised that 'my Māori friend' was, in a sense, a ghost, a creation of my memory. I had to admit to myself that, as a child, I did not really know Maria or even play with her much, and she barely knew me. All my adult life, I had traced my interest in Māori back to Maria, and the lively impact she had on me, as my friend. But it turned out she was barely my childhood friend at all. She was a fantasy of my own life story, making Dannevirke the place where my memories started.

Perhaps memory is sometimes made from desire. If that is so, my imagined memory of Maria makes sense. My parents' isolation, my mother's distraction, and the orderliness of my life attracted a memory of its opposite, warm togetherness in a busy house full of comings and goings, and activated my deep wish to belong. My memory was made of a childish longing for love and for home, two things I did not have, but which Māori – in the person of Maria – seemed to have in spades.

The next morning, I took Maria a coffee in her barbershop, next to the old Post Office – now closed due to earthquake risk – with its dusty Corinthian columns, and its large bronze clock stuck at ten to three. Business was okay, she said; she had her regulars, charged $20 for a standard cut, and gave free haircuts to people who were broke. Above a pile of rugby books for her customers to read was a corkboard crammed with photographs of her family, children, grandchildren, friends, and her favourite All Blacks. Her happy little white dog, Fleur, was outside, tied to an ancient gnarled weeping elm. I realised it was the same tree I stood beneath with my parents watching the Friday night marching bands more than fifty years before.

It was still early afternoon, but Maria locked the shop's front door, and turned the sign to Closed. Out the back, we leaned against the warm, sunny stone wall of the Post Office, facing the blue Ruahine ranges. She smiled in their direction: 'Aren't they beautiful!' I still found them oppressive; they were not my mountains. 'They *are* beautiful,' I agreed. Time seemed to stretch out into a past I was keen to revisit. She was happy to talk.

Before I met Maria in standard three, she had lived all her life at Kaitoke, a rural area south of Dannevirke. Her Ngāti Kahungunu relations lived in the neighbouring houses, and she recalls an idyllic childhood, riding her bike with her cousins and some Pākehā neighbours on the dirt roads, taking picnics to the local river, catching eels, sliding down hillsides, eating apples, plums and walnuts from the family orchards, and enjoying garden vegetables and watercress. The family went on the road with her shearer father and her head 'rousie' (fleece handler) mother for the three-month-long shearing contracts around the region. When she recently saw some photos of herself as a kid at Kaitoke, Maria was shocked: 'We looked like those slaves in the movies! Or refugees! Old clothes that did not fit, bare feet, and skinny ... but real happy.'

I realised that I had no sense of Maria's background. As a child I had admired her, and liked the Māori kids, but I knew nothing about them as Māori, that is, I had no idea about where

they came from tribally, or how colonial history had affected
them. So I asked Maria about her marae. In those days, the
word was usually pā, rather than marae. For Maria, her pā was
a hall. Some Ngāti Kahungunu families in the area, including
hers, built a Memorial Hall at Kaitoke following the Second
World War. The main Ngāti Kahungunu pā was miles away at
Mākirikiri, near Dannevirke, and this new hall was for everyone,
Māori and Pākehā. The hall was the centre of the Kaitoke
community – a place for birthdays, weddings, church, Sunday
School and tangihanga. People called it the pā, she says, but
it did not follow the rules of the meeting house on a marae
where food is strictly forbidden. Everyone ate inside the hall
before a separate dining room was built. Like the other children
around the pā, Maria made herself handy. She set and cleared
the tables for visitors and helped with the food and the dishes.
When she was very small, her father tied a long rope from her
waist to his leg to stop her wandering; people complained about
the rope tripping everyone up.

On special occasions, the Brethren Sunday School teachers,
Mr and Mrs Wall, would bring lemonade and cake to the pā:
'It was like the Ritz for us Māori kids! We just loved it.' The
Brethren gave out free booklets from the Maori Postal Sunday
School movement which produced English-language religious
tracts 'to reach and teach the many scattered Maori Children
throughout Maoriland with the pure Gospel and the Word
of God'.[1] I asked Maria if she still believed in a Christian God.
Without a pause, she said: 'Yes, that's how we were brought up.'
I remembered going with my family to the Dannevirke Anglican
church in town each Sunday, and singing in the church choir.
But I couldn't say 'that's how we were brought up'; it was just
something we did.

I asked Maria why her Mum and Dad left Kaitoke. I had a vague sense that many Māori were forced off their lands, but I did not know the details, or whether this was the case for Ngāti Kahungunu. Maria admitted she knew nothing about Māori land when she was a child playing sports at Dannevirke North School. Although her father spoke Māori at political meetings, she did not take much interest in politics, or the language. She had learned that Governor George Grey, as part of the massive Crown acquisition of Māori land all over the country in the 1850s, promised social and economic benefits if her Kahungunu people sold their lands to the Crown and gifted portions for schools. The people did this. But the promises of that kawenata (covenant) were not kept, and the iwi, under protest, lost most of its land and got little or nothing in return. For those remaining on the land, the rates were unaffordable and the building regulations complicated and inflexible. Many of her relations could not afford the costs of developing their land, so they moved into town and had to let the land go wild.

I recalled sitting in the back seat of the Plymouth staring through the window at the gorse- and thistle-covered paddocks around Dannevirke, and hearing my father's disdain for undeveloped 'Māori land' that was being 'wasted'. No doubt some of that land belonged to Maria's people who did not have the means to farm it. Maria continued: 'the land slowly went to the Pākehā. We Māori went along with it. Those Pākehā did not understand that they destroyed our culture and our way of life when they took that land.' Not only was the culture altered, I thought, as Maria spoke, but Māori lost their economic base. And the resulting poverty is at the root of so many modern Māori experiences.

In the early 1960s when I was in Dannevirke, rural Māori

were being actively encouraged to move to the towns. Barriers to developing rural kāinga – Māori villages – such as not being allowed to build a house unless the family owned at least 5 acres of land, forced Māori families into towns where state houses or sections could be purchased through the Department of Maori Affairs by capitalising the Family Benefit. Wanting their own house, Maria's parents had left their family land at Kaitoke to come in to Robert Street, a new state housing area in the town.

Maria recovered quickly from leaving her relations in the country because the Robert Street kids formed her new community; they played together in the street and swam in the nearby Mangatera Stream. 'The river was free, and when we came up the gully from the river, we'd get so hot we'd just run back down again for another swim!' Maria's brother and his friends dug a cave in the mud bank down in the gully and slept there one night. I remembered going down the Mangatera gully one weekend, hoping to see Maria there, but being too afraid of the big boys to approach the laughing, swinging, shouting gaggle of Māori children. My shyness added to the guilt I felt about disobeying my mother's instruction not to go down the gully ... was it because that's where the Māori kids were?

I asked Maria about her mother. Unlike my own mother who always demanded what she wanted from social institutions, Maria's mother did not expect much: 'She was just so grateful for anything she had. Life just happened.' Even when she lost an eye due to a neglectful doctor, she was never resentful. Maria remembers her mother as 'religious in an old-fashioned, accepting sort of way, and in times of difficulty would tell her children to recite the Lord's Prayer'. She used to say: 'The same sun shines on you, wherever you are. Whether rich or poor, we all live under the same sun.'

I kept talking with Maria about her life. She did not mind; in fact, she seemed glad to talk about things. What about te reo Māori? Maria was never encouraged to speak Māori, though as a child she heard her father speaking the language fluently at the pā. Under the influence of Māori and Pākehā politicians, and Rātana teachings that rejected Māori traditions, Maria's parents believed that 'going the Pākehā way' was the best future option. It was something she never really thought about at the time. Maria recalled waiata from her childhood, but reckoned she was too old now to learn the language.

————

It was late afternoon by the time our talk turned to local Māori politics. Maria is a member of the Kahungunu ki Wairarapa Tāmaki-nui-a-Rua Trust Board which has the mandate to negotiate with the Crown for a Treaty settlement. She confessed: 'I never thought about Māori politics until recently. I was too busy just surviving. And now I am learning all about it. I came back to Dannevirke a few years ago and – hello! – I'm on the Trust Board!'

Maria is now one of a group seeking He Kawenata Hou (a new covenant) with the government, whereby some land will be returned to Ngāti Kahungunu. She told me that they are getting only some tiny fragments back, but the process was exciting even if sometimes nasty. Not long ago, a group of her relations went to inspect an empty school property as part of the claim. A Pākehā neighbour confronted them aggressively, demanding to know why they were wandering around on that land. 'He looked down on us,' said Maria, 'just like in the old days.'

The afternoon sun was weakening. I felt exhausted after

our hours of talking. We decided to meet for one last time, the next day, before my return to Auckland. We would drive out to Kaitoke, her childhood home, and visit the pā.

———

I picked Maria up after breakfast and, leaving the little white dog tied up on her front lawn, we drove through the damp dairy country to the tiny settlement of Kaitoke. I parked near the hall, and we sat on the wooden benches in the front porch where the Sunday School teachers once delighted Maria and her relations with delicious cake. These days younger kura-educated Māori women argue with Maria about the hall's protocols. Maria allows eating inside the porch and the hall, something forbidden by a younger generation who call the Memorial Hall their wharenui. They try to tell her the correct Māori way: when to pōwhiri, how to hongi, where to eat. 'I learned from my mother and aunties from around here,' Maria said, 'That's good enough for me. I just ignore them and do it my way.' I snorted in sympathy, and imagined how we must look: two older women sitting together comfortably in front of an old hall in the middle of nowhere, laughing.

As women sometimes do, we talked about marriage. I took from my bag my battered 1964 autograph book. In it, Maria had written in neat pencil a common girlish ditty: 'To Alison. Alison for now, Alison for ever, Jones for now, but not for ever. From Maria.' Maria asked if I had ever changed my name, and when I replied 'Never! I'm a staunch feminist!' she sat back, surveying the grass in front of the hall: 'I was like that once. Staunch. Feminist. But then I fell in love and I thought everything would be different. We would be a Mum and Dad and make a family like my parents did, and Wayne and I would get old together. I even took his name. He went off with someone else.' She went on: 'I was earning good money in Wellington, but something did not feel right – *do you understand that?* – so I came home ... I had lost myself, and got myself back. I had to come back here, back home.'

She sat quite still, and I was left with her question 'Do you understand that?' My own sense of place is different. I had left Dannevirke's darkly mysterious mountains, and never wanted to return. And I have no ancient history rooted in any particular New Zealand landscape; I love it all. I particularly love my city, Auckland. I feel constantly the pull of the friends and family and the work I have there, the cafés and parks, the sparkling harbour and the wild sea. Of course, I nod, I understand. But I am not so sure I do.

———

I realise now, writing this, that I have spent a lot of time going over my relationship with Maria. Childhood is where our emotions are anchored, and where memories (real and imagined) are most vivid. When I left Dannevirke and Maria, I left my childhood to become an adolescent. But those childhood memories remained, leaving deeper traces the further I went into my adult life.

Māori on the front lawn

Whakatāne. A town by the head of a river, in a place with a magical name: Bay of Plenty. Arriving there from Dannevirke was like coming up to the light. The clouds were buoyant and fluffy: seaside clouds. The sky was sea-blue.

Whakatāne's sweet air quickly banished memories of the damp and musty Dannevirke; under its wide-open sky, my adolescent imagination filled with possibility. It was the beginning of summer, and my mother and father and we five children moved in to a small house near the hospital where Dad was to work as an accountant. I was now eleven, and becoming self-conscious about my place in the world. In Whakatāne, I would be a smaller fish in a bigger pond – and, I noticed, it was a much more Māori pond.

I have a strong memory of the first time I went into the centre of town. As in most New Zealand riverside towns, the shops kept their backs to the water, and their shady front verandahs stretched invitingly along the single main street, the Strand. My parents had encouraged the twins and me to explore. We left our bikes outside the Post Office in the metal bike racks and, like three mildly alarmed sheep, we walked in a small bunch along the shop fronts.

Two moments stand out. One was my discovery of Pōhaturoa, an imposing rock, the size of a four-storey house, which stood opposite the library. The local iwi, Ngāti Awa, once put ancestral bones into Pōhaturoa's sacred crevices. Apparently, the Whakatāne River had flowed past its feet, but land reclamation for the shops had left it high and dry. It was an odd thing: an enormous, jagged, lichen- and tree-covered rock, right in the middle of town.

Then I noticed the women. In the shade of the verandahs, sitting against the shop fronts, they were as surely and solidly positioned as Pōhaturoa. I herded my siblings before me, gazing at the half-dozen old Māori women who sat side by side, wearing black and wrapped in dark blankets. A couple of them smoked pipes. Most had dark tattoos, moko kauae, on their chins. A few small children sat among them and a sleeping baby lay in one lap.

The group gave no attention to passers-by, but to a young girl who had never seen people sitting on a pavement, these women were a revelation. I wanted to stop and listen to their gentle conversation, even though I could not understand a word. I tried not to stare at them. Who were they? Where did they come from? They seemed to inhabit themselves completely, and to link the present with the past in a way I could not explain.

I saw the women again on the Strand a few times at the end of 1964 and into 1965, sometimes just two or three at a time. Then, they stopped coming. They were probably Ngāti Awa people, having come in from inland villages such as Tāneatua and Te Teko, to shop and to talk. I did not know then that these women were the last of the old world, and that I was lucky to have seen them.

———

It was here that my parents got their first mortgage. Our bungalow on Commerce St looked not unlike the dream house on the Dannevirke butcher's calendar. It was pretty, with decorative shutters, and its spacious yard backed onto a scrub-covered hillside that overlooked the town. A neatly mowed front lawn accommodated a large phoenix palm.

Next door lived Dr and Mrs Maaka. They had chooks, and my mother had two cocker spaniels. We kids had to make sure that the dogs did not get in to the Maakas' back garden and chase the chooks. Needless to say, the dogs found any gap in the hedge and our apologies to Mrs Maaka were embarrassingly frequent. Mrs Maaka's first name was Florence, and my mother chatted over the fence with her first Māori acquaintance. When my brother saw a spectre one night in the hall of our house, Mum consulted Mrs Maaka. Mrs Maaka explained to Mum the ghost was that of a previous inhabitant. Mrs Maaka's confident assertion made the ghost real to our family. Somehow, her being Māori gave her access to that other world.

I was aware of my mother talking to Mrs Maaka in a way I did not notice her doing with Mrs Limmer, a Pākehā neighbour. Mrs Maaka, she reported, was 'lovely!' A visiting Māori tradesman had 'such beautiful handwriting!' A Māori nurse 'had a lovely smile, and did a very good job!' Her exaggerated enthusiasms served to underline for me her uncertainty about how to interact with Māori. She seemed surprised by Māori competence, which she felt compelled to encourage. I was embarrassed by this, and dreaded meeting a Māori person in her company in case she was gushy.

I did not know then that Mrs Maaka's husband was famous. Dr Golan (Te Korana) Haberfield Maaka was one of the first Māori to graduate in medicine, and he had worked in China.

He saw his patients in the front room of his house, where we children went for our vaccinations. Dr Maaka did not charge fees, relying on the government subsidy, and he had a huge number of Māori patients, many of whom would bring him a feed of potatoes or a dozen beer. Dr Maaka's patients taught him the use of rongoā (herbal cures), which he combined with Chinese and Western medicine. I learned later that he dealt with many cases of mākutu, or bewitching, by advising victims to visit the local tohunga.

Dr Maaka's patients interested me. Most of them came to see him on the weekends, when they took up residence on our front lawn. On Saturdays, I would gaze out through the net curtains of our living room at the remarkable sight of large groups of Māori sitting on blankets under the shade of the phoenix palm, their food in pots and boxes. Kids ran about on the grass that Dad had meticulously mowed. These visitors had travelled from the surrounding districts, and would wait, chatting and joking, sometimes for hours, until family members had seen the doctor.

My mother tolerated the people on the lawn, though she never spoke to them, or offered food or water. I studied them from the window, entranced by their easy engagement with each other, and the fact that they comfortably claimed our lawn without asking. The yearning I felt as I looked through the curtains was not a desire to be among them; I was touched instead by that same longing I had in Maria's house in Dannevirke, for a shared family life, with aunties and uncles and cousins, and laughter.

One Saturday, as I studied the group from my secret observation post, a small child from amongst them ran out on to the road. The adults did not move but shouted sharply at one

of the older children who immediately dashed out, grabbed the
toddler and returned him into the centre of the picnickers. As
far as I could see, nothing more was said, not even a growling
or a thanks; the adults simply went on eating and talking. I was
astonished; in my family, the parents would have jumped up in
panic and admonished the child with a smack and a long lecture
about road safety.

———

About this time, we got our first television set. Among our
favourite shows from the United States – *Bewitched*, *Get
Smart* and *The Andy Griffith Show* – was the occasional New
Zealand programme. One winter afternoon, I watched a rare
Māori performance on *Songs of their Forefathers*. I adored the
melodious waiata and the graceful poi, and the haka enthralled
me. My father walked into the living room and abruptly
switched off the set. 'Why did you do that?' I was annoyed.
'Seen one, you've seen them all,' was all he said. I remember this
moment because – once again – I was confirmed in my shocking
realisation that my father could be wrong. It was becoming
painfully clear to me that he and I inhabited different worlds.

In Whakatāne, our house was heavy with a mysterious
tension. My parents' bedroom door was often locked shut,
muffling secret conversations. I learned later that my father's
depression had intensified. I must have intuited this, because
out of the blue one day I expressed the unsaid: 'I think I am
depressed.' 'You do not know what depression is,' said my
mother, accurately, in a hard voice. I disliked her for that, with
adolescent vehemence. She was not prepared to ask why I felt
that way, or why I had uttered that embarrassing word. Now

I know she was exhausted by my father's puzzling, shameful illness; any indication of neediness from me, her reliable lieutenant, must have been difficult for her to bear.

Adding to the stress, I later learned, my father became infatuated with another woman. In those days there was no benefit for single mothers; if our breadwinner had left, we would have been destitute. Through sheer force of personality – perhaps invoking his guilt, or a sense of duty – my mother forbade my father to leave our household. Her orphanage upbringing had honed her survival instincts; she was difficult to disobey. We children knew nothing of all this, except for sensing an unnerving and unnamed tension.

School was my haven. I was happy there, amongst the boisterous kids. At Apanui Primary, where I started in February 1965, the military habits from a war that had ended twenty years before still shaped the start of the school day. All the children lined up in our 'house' groups (mine was Rimu) and marched around the grassy playground behind banners. Jaunty military music blared out from two horn-like loudspeakers fixed above a classroom block. I loved the rhythmic beat; it united us all with a shared purpose. Three abreast, we had to stay in step, even through the 'eyes right' command as we passed the headmaster standing, like an old commander, in front of the school buildings. Most of the kids loved the routine, and the boys squabbled over whose turn it was to carry the house banner.

The principal was a short, benign Pākehā man named Mr Richards. He had only one arm; the other, we heard, was 'shot off during the war in the desert'. This always seemed wonderfully romantic to me, and I regarded Mr Richards with solemn respect for his overseas war adventures.

———

When I turned twelve, I got an after-school job at the public library. One of the library assistants was Lita, who came from the Pacific. I do not know whether she was Samoan, Niuean or Tongan – in those days, such differences were rarely acknowledged by Europeans. I liked her a lot, and I enjoyed her motherly lessons on such topics as the evils of cigarettes, as we sat, and she smoked, on the library's back steps during her break. One afternoon, Lita took a clean handkerchief from her bag and inhaled a cigarette through it. She held up the white cotton to show me the tarry, dark stain left by the smoke.

When I reported this to my mother, she screwed up her nose and said Lita 'must have had blood on her lips'. I was perplexed by this odd response. Maybe she was just defending her own smoking habit, to keep my judgment at bay. Her reference to blood disgusted me, and something about its vivid crudeness made me suspect her reaction was to Lita's being Polynesian.

My mother's indifference – or mild hostility – towards my discoveries and delights turned me away from her. I would lie alone spreadeagled on our back lawn, my back against the cool earth, staring up at the evening stars. Or I would climb the hill behind the house through the dusty bracken to a large pōhutukawa tree, where I would gaze out at the beautiful township of Whakatāne, its winding river, and the sparkling sea beyond, with its large humped whale-shaped island Whale Island (Moutohorā), and the steaming live volcano White Island (Whakaari) off in the distance. I could see to the firm dark line of the horizon. I was a giant, looking out over the tiny cars and houses of my domain.

Up above the town and the sea, I could wonder, and dream.

I sometimes thought about the history of the land before
me. I was troubled by a story I had heard at Girl Guides. A
local historian, Clive Kingsley-Smith, had told us that the
lands around Whakatāne had been taken from Māori. He had
explained that because the Ngāti Awa people from this district
had tried to resist the Pākehā who wanted land, the whole area
was confiscated by the government.[1] Mr Kingsley-Smith had
taken us to the small lock-up in Toroa Street that, he told us,
once held Māori resisters. I imagined the little building darkly
crowded with angry men and, even though I barely understood
the history, I felt great pity for them. He told us that Ngāti
Awa once owned flour mills, and hired Pākehā shipbuilders to
make ships to carry wheat, flour, flax, pigs, sheep, timber and
potatoes to the markets in Auckland.[2] After the land confiscations, the people of Ngāti Awa were reduced to working for the
Pākehā, who built houses, factories, farms and shops on their
ancestral lands.

All these things worried me in a way I could not quite put
my finger on. I was confused by the idea of confiscation, and I
wondered about the fate of the Māori people who once lived
here. I did not yet make the connection between the story of
Ngāti Awa's land loss and the elderly women under the shop
verandahs, the picnickers on our front lawn, the Māori kids at
school or the fact that Māori were the labouring people of the
district, working on land that now belonged to Pākehā. I did
not know the iwi names then, and all the 'stories of the Māori'
I heard at school or in books were mythical tales, or set in the
distant past. Even Mr Kingsley-Smith's stories were from a
past that seemed as remote as Noah's Ark. The Māori kids, the
streets and houses and shops of Whakatāne were now simply
present. No one around me ever mentioned their history, so

my nebulous worries never cohered into knowledge. Most Pākehā, unlike Mr Kingsley-Smith, seemed to have forgotten Whakatāne's past. My parents, certainly, did not have a clue.

———

As well as withdrawing from my troubled parents, I was busy alienating my younger sister Gillian. Jealous of her prettiness, and confused about how to be likeable while maintaining a sharp, critical mind, I was alternately nice and horrible. Gillian and I shared a bedroom, and I would crawl under the blankets to lie very still, pretending to have suffocated to death. Gillian's crying would prompt me to leap out and laugh. I was bursting with unanswered questions about life, and channelled my energy into teasing her – and other girls I considered soft – by menacing them with handfuls of wriggling worms and slaters or alienating them with taunting jibes. These petty cruelties hurt my sister, who just wanted to be my friend; I pushed her away, to be alone on the edge of my own alternative world.

All my brothers and sisters, I now think, felt isolated from each other – perhaps giving expression to our parents' secret domestic problems, their respective personal anxieties, and their marooning as immigrants without an extended family on these islands. My youngest sister developed epilepsy (she became famous for a spectacular seizure one morning at school assembly), and our fearful father wrapped his cloak of conservatism more tightly around him, angrily suppressing the children's opinions at dinner-table conversations.

On weekend evenings, my mother worked at the hospital switchboard, and I made cheese on toast for the family meal. I did not particularly enjoy the responsibility, and disliked Mum's abandoning us to our gloomy father. As our parents became increasingly unhappy, Dad with his mysterious depression and Mum with her despair over her husband's illness, we children did not turn to each other. We turned away, each on our own, in different directions.

Despite all this, I have very happy memories of Whakatāne. Mum and Dad kept up outward appearances, and we children were allowed to roam freely. I spent a lot of time down at the heads of the river, riding there on my bike. Fat juicy cherries grew in our backyard, I had a beloved budgie trained to sit on my shoulder and, with money from my job at the library, I could buy a secret stash of my favourite malt barley sugars. And I made two good friends from vastly different backgrounds.

Two friends

At Apanui School in Whakatāne, a vivacious Māori girl named Jackie became my friend at first sight. She was in my class, and I thought she was the most beautiful girl I had ever seen. Her broad, open face had a diffidence and vulnerability that I was drawn to. She had a strength of personality that matched my own, and she seemed happy to be my best friend.

Jackie, like the sporty, adventurous Maria in Dannevirke, had dark skin and wavy black hair. She and her younger sister and brother lived with their father, who was a driver for the Whakatāne Board Mills. He was a talented musician, and (I was very impressed by this) he had not a single filling in his teeth. Most interesting to me – and unusual for that time – was the fact that Jackie's mother did not live with the family.

Jackie's house, rented from her father's employer, was near ours, and she and I walked home from school together and visited each other's houses. At the weekends, we would often ride side-by-side on our bikes down to the mouth of the Whakatāne River, a place known as 'the heads', where the sea pounded over a sandbar. On a high, wild rock where the river meets the sea was a new bronze statue of a slim young woman teetering on tiptoe as if about to dive in to the water, her long, hard hair standing out horizontally behind her like a rope.

At school, we had learned the story of this teenager, Wairaka, brave daughter of the rangatira Toroa, who saved the Ngāti Awa ancestral waka, *Mataatua*, on its arrival in New

Zealand. The men had made it to shore but the waka, with the women and children aboard, was being pulled out to sea by the raging waves. Wairaka called out 'Kia whakatāne au i ahau!' (I must act like a man!). She grabbed the paddles, which only men were permitted to use, and the other women followed her lead. Together they manoeuvred the heavy waka to safety right there at the river mouth.

The bronze Wairaka was small and slight, and I wondered how she could have taken control of a massive canoe. Nevertheless, both Jackie and I felt proud of her deeds, which had given the town its name. On the shore, Jackie balanced in the same pose as the bronze statue so I could compare a modern girl with one from long ago.

Tourists occasionally took photographs of us as we mucked around on the sandy riverbank. I was self-conscious enough to wonder if their attention had something to do with the idea – or ideal – of a Māori and a Pākehā child playing together. It was 1965, and concepts of race and race relations were getting regular global attention. As well as stories about the North American Black Liberation movement, the New Zealand relationship with apartheid South Africa was regularly in the news. Our rugby teams touring South Africa had, since the 1920s, excluded Māori players to save the South Africans the embarrassment of hosting non-white people, and opposition to rugby bosses' craven capitulation to this requirement had gathered pace in the 1960s. The implication that Māori rugby players could not go to South Africa because they were deemed to be black or coloured I found odd – partly because skin colour seemed so irrelevant to sport, and partly because Māori were clearly not African or Indian.

Although my youthful analysis rather missed the point,

I started to understand that, whether I liked it or not, I was a member of a dominant (white) group that was being unfair and even violent towards black and brown people around the world. The descriptor 'white', now firmly linked to bad behaviour, filled me with ambivalence and confusion.

I have one quite vivid memory of my growing unease about 'race'. At the school gate was a tiny slatted shed, into which metal crates of milk were delivered each morning. In those days, the government supplied half-pint glass bottles of milk to every schoolchild. We were under pressure to drink the milk at playtime after it had warmed in the crate for a couple of hours. I dreaded having to force down that vile, fatty liquid and did everything I could to avoid it. Anyway, after school one day, Jackie and I decided to frighten the younger children. Jackie got into the empty shed and, crawling behind the vertical slats, pretended to be a savage, growling as the kids walked past. I stood nearby issuing urgent warnings about the cannibal in the crate. I must have been convincing because the children gave it a wide berth. Even though Jackie was an enthusiastic participant, I was faintly aware that her being both a Māori and the savage made our game shameful, and was pleased when it came to an end and we could walk home along the footpath as two normal girls, laughing about our trick.

In 1968, Jackie and I were confirmed in the Anglican Church (there was a photograph in the *Whakatane Beacon* of us together, demure in virginal white), and we both became school prefects. We stopped playing silly games and tried to be grown-up, walking about the school with prefect badges on our budding chests, or lying on Ōhope Beach on the weekends in our bikinis. Although we enjoyed our teenage time together, I sensed that Jackie was unhappy. But she maintained a gritty cheerfulness, even though she always had plenty of chores, and responsibility for her two younger siblings. She had to get in the family's washing from the line and prepare the meat, potatoes and vegetables that her father would cook when he got home from work, and she worried when her younger sister did not come straight home from school. Like Maria, Jackie seemed older than me in terms of domestic experience, and my admiration for her strengthened our friendship.

———

I eventually lost touch with Jackie and, writing this book, I was keen to meet her again. I noticed from news reports that she was active in Māori land-claim politics. I found her on social media and she agreed to meet me at her home in Tauranga. I took a stack of old school photos with me, and on a grey winter's day, we sat together at her kitchen table, remembering our primary school days. At first, she seemed reluctant to talk about the past. She talked instead about her children and grandchildren, and her Christian faith. Gradually, as we chatted, the warmth of our old friendship returned.

Jackie remembered her first sight of me at school. I wore a brown paisley dress, she said, with a rolled collar and a white pattern on the front, and I carried a brown leather satchel, though I have no memory of this. 'You were all prepared!' Jackie recalled, smiling. She liked me immediately. I remember feeling the same way about her.

We talked about the shape of our lives, and she told me that, on the advice of her secondary school teachers, she had gone to Canterbury University. She ended up training as a primary school teacher, meeting her future husband, a man active in university Māori politics. At university, she recalls, she 'went through the process of decolonisation' and 'became Māori'. In stage one lectures, she learned about 'Pākehā settlement and the history of Māori land' from the historian David McIntyre. Māori activists such as Dun Mihaka, Tame Iti and Koro Dewes were campaigning for Māori rights and language. She met her father's sister again, and found lost whānau connections. She learned about tikanga. For the first time in her life, she admitted, she felt a sense of purpose.

I asked Jackie about 'being Māori' at school. She did not really think of herself as Māori. But a memory still burns. It was, she said, during a reading lesson in standard three about the Māori leader and prophet Te Kooti. During the attacks and upheavals of the late nineteenth century, Te Kooti made powerful enemies amongst Māori and Pākehā by fighting both alongside, and against, government troops. In Pākehā histories he was a violent rebel, and this was the story taught in primary school. As a child, Jackie's unhappy calculation was that 'he was a Māori, like me, and he came from a place near Whakatāne. If he was a baddie then I must be, too.' She remembered crying with hurt and humiliation, unable to explain her feelings to a sympathetic teacher. In form two, when some friends spoke negatively about Māori, she told them 'But I'm Māori!' The considered reply was 'yes, but you're different.' These experiences, Jackie said, 'separated me out from the Pākehā kids a bit.'

I was curious about her mother and Jackie explained the sad story. She adored her mother, even when she wore embarrassingly short skirts, long beads, and eye makeup on school visits. She was a beautiful, independent Māori woman who earned her own money as a hospital cleaning supervisor. She wore fashionable shoes, sewed lovely dresses for Jackie, knitted for the family and loved cooking. She took Jackie to Plunket events, and to tap-dancing lessons, where Jackie was the only Māori child. She and Jackie travelled to dance competitions in other towns, where they ate in restaurants, stayed in hotels, and went to the movies. It was, says Jackie, 'a magical life'.

Then, without warning, when Jackie was eight years old, her beloved, beautiful mother left: 'One day she was there; the next she was gone.' She had gone to live with another man. Jackie was heartbroken. Things were made worse when Jackie's mother tried to see her children against their father's wishes. Jackie's father was dealing with the situation on his own. He refused to let the children see their mother's family.

Jackie remembered feeling quite alone, separated from her mother's Te Arawa whānau. She loved coming to my house as a child because 'you were a normal, happy family. You had a mother who stayed at home and cooked and sewed, and your house was orderly and quiet. Your father and mother were kind to me.'

I was amused, and surprised, at her recollection of my family. As children, it seems, we each wanted something of the other's life. I had found my home's order and quiet oppressive. To escape it, I liked going to Jackie's house. There, we kids sat close together on their low couch, singing with gusto while Jackie's father played his guitar. At those moments, I felt happily contented. My family never sang together or listened to shared music, though I was unenthusiastically learning the piano (something Jackie wanted to do; I taught her the piano tune 'Für Elise', and she practised its finger patterns on her bedroom wall). Our tastefully papered living-room walls were not as exciting as the abstract murals that Jackie's mother had once painted on theirs. Jackie had found the ordinariness of our nuclear family a relief from the confusing sadness of her own, while for me the warmth at her house was an escape from my parents' controlling worries and expectations.

———

Our lives diverged at secondary school. Jackie and I were channelled into different streams. I went into 3L (the L was for Latin, which we learned in addition to French). This was the top of the school's ten streams in a careful academic ranking arranged from the 'bright' to the 'average' down to the 'not-so-gifted', as the principal put it in his 1967 annual report.[1]

Jackie had done well at primary school, and she, too, opted to take Latin. But at the enrolment interview, she told me later, her request was met with 'No. One foreign language will be enough for you.' Her father did not know to argue on Jackie's behalf, so she found herself in the next class down, separated from her closest friends, including me. I was mystified at what I thought had been Jackie's own choice. In a school where one-third of the students were Māori, only one Māori child, a doctor's daughter, made it into 3L.

Through my first year at high school, at my mother's insistence, I continued to write letters to my English grand-mother, a woman who existed for me only in photographs. She had a pale, elderly, faded look, even though she would have been only in her mid-sixties, and I felt no kinship with her. The letters, which my uncle gave me years later, confronted me with the fact that I sometimes imagined myself to be a middle-class English schoolgirl. Just before my fourteenth birthday I wrote in a neat cursive hand:

Dear Gran. When I have finished this letter, I am going to attempt some Latin verbs. When I started Latin, I had an awful bother trying to learn the stuff! But I think I've got the 'hang' of it now. Did you ever learn Latin? Its horrid!!

The language of the letter with its self-conscious inverted commas, and its multiple exclamation marks, embarrass me now. At the same time, I have some compassion for my teenage self: a daughter of immigrants attempting to navigate an independent female identity, at the same time trying to impress my grandmother by reflecting – in laughably stereotypical language straight from English comic books – what I imagined were her cultural ways.

———

Whakatāne High School was full of confident Pākehā kids who had read more than I had and who knew more about world affairs, and English, and maths. In 3L, I immediately befriended my potential academic rival, Vivienne. One of her attractive qualities was her family's house. She lived on a spectacular headland above the grand sweep of Ōhope Beach over the hill from Whakatāne. The large house was in a 1950s estate built for North American executives establishing the Tasman Pulp and Paper mills and the mill town of Kawerau.

Vivienne and I spent weekends roaming about the headland, climbing up and down the old grass-covered Māori fortifications that had once been part of a series of pā. We did not know it, but the headland area was once the heartland of the Ngāti Awa people, with thriving pā and rich fishing grounds, and crevices that held the bones of the ancestors.

Being a young Pākehā girl with other things on her mind, I

did not feel the ghosts of the Ngāti Awa people on this beautiful
clifftop. But one Sunday morning we encountered a group of
Māori at the top of the steep track that led down to a secluded
bay near her house. We were setting off for the beach, towels
around our shoulders, when an old car pulled up, and about
six people tumbled out, with hessian sacks and diving masks.
I had never seen Māori in this posh neighbourhood and for an
instant I wondered if they were allowed here. As they rushed
past us, alarmingly exuberant, one of the men turned and
grinned, raising his eyebrows in greeting. I suddenly felt as
though *we* were trespassing, as we climbed down to the pebbly
bay. Now, knowing that the people were heading to a traditional
fishing spot near an area that was once wholly theirs, I know my
instincts were correct: in a sense we were on their territory.

Vivienne's house was large and fully carpeted (a sure
sign of affluence). She and her three siblings each had their
own bedroom, and the family owned a wonderful record
collection. Vivienne's father was in the real-estate business.
Most surprising and enjoyable to me, unlike the repressed
atmosphere in my home where my father dismissed children's
opinions, Vivienne's family seriously debated news of the day
at the dinner table. Through 1967 and 1968, we talked about the
war in Vietnam, the shocking assassination of Martin Luther
King in Memphis, Tennessee, as well as fashion and rock and
roll. I do not recall having clear political views, then. I was hazy
about who Martin Luther King actually was, and exactly why I
should oppose the Vietnam War, but I loved to be part of a lively
family conversation.

In a bubble of teenage happiness, Vivienne and I listened
to the latest music hits by Herman's Hermits, Sandie Shaw,
and the Rolling Stones ('Kids are different today/I hear every

mother say'). Even in the small town of Whakatāne, we sensed the youth-led rebellion sweeping the Western world. Everything had intense potency; I could feel myself growing up. Time seemed to quicken, and I wanted it all to slow down. Before I went to bed each night in the room I shared with my sister, I tied a knot in a length of orange wool, imagining each day held tight there forever. I kept the ever-shortening strand of wool in a special place in my top drawer.

Soon, yet again, my father felt compelled to move. Perhaps to distract himself again from his persistent and intensifying depression, he took another accounting job, this time at the Tauranga Harbour Board. None of the rest of us wanted to leave Whakatāne. Miserably, we packed up the Plymouth again, and drove to the city of Tauranga, about 50 miles west along the Bay of Plenty coast.

I was fifteen years old. My mother persuaded me to give away my dolls, my friends signed my school Panama hat with self-consciously practised signatures, and I threw away the knotted orange wool with happy adolescent days bound into its strands.

Area returned
to the Natives

We rented a small house on the edge of the grey-blue Tauranga harbour, near a spooky, scraggy pile of sand and mud, covered with wattle, that the local kids called Rat Island (it was known to Māori as Motuopuhi, which suggests an illustrious history, maybe an island where young women went). It was summer and Tauranga should have felt like a good place to be. But nothing went well.

The old two-bedroom cottage was so tiny that at night we children lay in sleeping bags on camp beds jammed up against each other. I befriended a neighbour my age in order to learn to sail his small yacht until, out on the water, he tried to kiss me with wet lips. In an accident in another boy's car, I was slightly injured and had to keep a badly bruised arm hidden from my parents. My brother wondered what it felt like to hang, and tied a rope noose around his own neck; he pulled on the rope and passed out, recovering enough for my mother to shout at him in relief. Heavy-duty epilepsy medication dulled and bewildered my bright little sister; it was my job to keep her company when she had what Mum called a 'turn'. My pretty sister developed bad acne and lay on her camp bed, her shining pimples to the wall, weeping miserably. My own acne muted any satisfaction I might have felt at her misfortune.

Towards the end of summer, we moved to a nearby rural village named Bethlehem. The house, on Carmichaels Road, was on a quarter-acre, between what we called Putt's Paddock and the Bethlehem School. My brothers and sisters and I liked our new house, with its large cheerful garden, and we were all happy to live in the countryside.

We were warned about petty theft in the neighbourhood. Our house's previous owners had been a white Rhodesian couple, probably refugees from the armed insurgencies roiling their native country after its unilateral declaration of independence from Britain in 1965. They had recommended to my mother that we position a stuffed reptile at the gate – 'It's supposed to scare Māoris away,' Mum said vaguely – though she never did it and nothing got stolen.

———

I enrolled at Tauranga Girls' College where, to my alarm, I was placed not in the top class, but in the second stream. My mother promptly marched off to the college to remonstrate. The deputy principal was a stern woman, but she relented and gave me a term in the top class 'to prove my worth'. Desperate to stay there, I crammed every minute with study. I was a slave to the school's demands, driven by my mother's disappointment about her own truncated schooling and her desires for my academic success. That year I gained a maths prize, and came second in biology and chemistry. Burdened by anxiety about academic achievement, I was miserable.

With money earned by gardening for neighbours, my sister and I bought records, and listened on the radio to the protest songs of the time. Donovan sang, 'He's the universal soldier and he really is to blame', and Joan Baez's rendition of Bob Dylan's 'Blowin' in the Wind' ('How many ears must one woman have before she can hear people cry?') filled me with unanswerable questions. The television scenes of the muddy, mad Woodstock concert in 1969 were thrilling; political protests in the United States showed up on our nightly news; London was in the midst of the Swinging Sixties: the model Twiggy's defiant steady gaze was like a two-finger salute to the adult generation. I identified with being 'against'; I just could not always identify exactly what I was against. It seemed that *everything* was wrong.

Much to my mother's consternation, above the desk in my bedroom, I pinned a swirling crimson-and-yellow poster with the words 'Damn everything but the circus' – a phrase from a lecture by the poet e.e. cummings:

> Damn everything but the circus! ... damn everything that
> is grim, dull, motionless, unrisking, inward turning, damn
> everything that won't get into the circle, that won't enjoy.
> That won't throw its heart into the tension, surprise,
> fear and delight of the circus, the round world, the full
> existence ...[1]

Damn everything that is grim, dull, inward turning! And yet – and I was ashamed of my natural conformity – I remained studious and obedient. School's inherent contradictions kept me in turmoil; in its outward turning, I learned about the marvels of poetry and the atom, and at the same time, its inward turning meant tests and examinations made every marvel into a grim, dull grade.

In English classes, I revelled in the words of Gerard Manley Hopkins as he pushed and pulled my imagination, immersing me in new observations of the world, light and dark, couple-colour, the dappled things.

Glory be to God for dappled things –
For skies of couple-colour as a brinded cow;
For rose-moles all in stipple upon trout that swim;
Fresh-firecoal chestnut-falls; finches' wings ...[2]

Hopkins' words had familiar echoes of my parents' land –
known, but also completely unknown to me – of chestnuts and
brinded cows. I found it harder to love James K. Baxter's desire
for:

... the eater of life, Hine-nui-te-pō,
With teeth of obsidian and hair like kelp
Flashing and glimmering at the edge of the horizon[3]

Baxter's poetry made me uncomfortable: the 'teeth of obsidian
and hair like kelp' was the hard, dark reality of here. Baxter
visited my school, and I remember scowling disapprovingly
at his scruffy, lank-haired, barefooted presence, as only a
judgmental adolescent girl could. He inflamed the tension in my
doubled self. I felt the close presence of the black hard obsidian
and the grasping kelp, but I yearned for the softly dappled
things.

———

My mixed feelings about Māori were at the heart of this tension
for me. Our house in Bethlehem was located near two pā and
their scattering of houses, each on its ancient waterway: one
to the north, on the harbour end of Bethlehem Road, and one
to the west, next to the Wairoa River. All I knew was that there
was a pā in that direction, and another pā in the other direction,
and that the Bethlehem pā kids got on our school bus each

morning in light-hearted scuffling crowds. The bus stop was right outside our gate. My sister remembers her fear of waiting with the Māori kids, sensing suppressed hostility towards us, the only Pākehā kids at the stop. All I remember are the Māori boys shoving at each other over some private disagreement, or fighting with their fists, getting sticky and grubby from wrestling in the paspalum at the dusty roadside.

I do not recall outright hostility, but there seemed to be an invisible wall between Māori and Pākehā. The Māori kids sat together on the bus, and the few Pākehā kids tended to sit in a group as well. It was Māori humour that bridged the unspoken divide. The Māori kids were always making jokes. My (Pākehā) boyfriend always saved me a seat near the back of the bus, and my passage down the crowded aisle was often accompanied by their mocking chorus of 'Here comes the bride', punctuated by laughing and whistling. My boyfriend's father owned a chicken farm along the route, and he was welcomed with clucking noises each morning as he boarded. I realise now that there was probably an invitation in the mockery; we Pākehā were being invited by the Māori kids to laugh with them, across the distance between us.

Although I knew one of the girls from Bethlehem pā, it never occurred to me that I could visit her there. And my mother showed no interest in getting to know the Māori families who lived up and down our road. I think she still felt, like most other Pākehā, that 'we didn't naturally mix, they kept to themselves.' The rare interactions didn't always go well. One afternoon a Māori child, playing with my brother on the road outside our house, fell off the bicycle, badly scraping his knee. He wailed so much that my mother took him by the hand down a long dirt track opposite our house, looking for his family. A group sitting along their front verandah regarded my approaching mother in silence. Mum later recalled feeling anxious about 'a strong us-and-them feeling'. Someone called out angrily, 'What's he done now?' Feeling that her care for the crying, bloodied child had been misconstrued, my mother silently handed him over and walked away. 'They treated me like I was the police,' she told me.

During a period when I had time off school to study, I developed a crush on a local Māori boy who worked as a caretaker in the school next door. I would contrive to be out in our garden trimming the hedge or inspecting the flowerbeds when he was in the school grounds, and we struck up shy conversations. I do not know why our budding relationship failed to develop, but I do recall thinking he was both wonderfully mysterious and utterly unattainable; this was underscored by the fact that he was from the well-known local Rewiti family. And I do know that my father would not have approved of my dating a Māori boy.

For my brothers, the situation could sometimes be dangerous. Not long after we arrived in the district, my brother Richard was dragged off his bicycle on Bethlehem Road and punched badly: 'That's for being a Park-ya [Pākehā],' his young Māori attackers yelled. My younger brother, Garrick, too, was targeted. He was about eight, a kind boy, with blond hair, and one of the few Pākehā kids at Bethlehem School. He soon dreaded going to school. His lunch was often stolen, he was constantly threatened or pushed about by Māori boys who called out sharp threats: 'Park-ya, give me 10 cents or I'll bash ya!' and 'Shut up you Park-ya or I'll strap your lips!' The violence was not only visited on Pākehā. Vicious fights would often erupt in the playground among the Māori boys: 'You're blacker than me!' 'Nah, you're the blackest!'

Even his Māori teacher was hostile in petty ways. While writing on the board, Garrick recalls, the teacher said 'Māori is spelt with a capital M, and Pākehā is spelt with a small p' and turned to stare meaningfully at Garrick, while the class sniggered. Intimidated and unhappy, Garrick left, and began cycling a long way each morning with his older brother – who would not get on the school bus – to a school in town.

Preoccupied with study, and dreaming complicated dreams of rose-moles all in stipple upon trout that swim, and damn everything but the circus, and teeth of obsidian and hair like kelp, flashing and glimmering, I knew little of my brothers' troubles. And I certainly did not wonder why the Māori kids might be hostile towards us, or towards each other.

———

To earn some pocket money, I would be up at dawn to cycle around the neighbourhood hurling rolled-up newspapers into the driveways of the sleeping houses. On our side, the south side of Carmichaels Road, the few Pākehā houses were modern, large and well built. On the north side, the houses belonging to Māori were usually small, some with toilet sheds out the back, and some without electricity. I watched an elderly man wash every morning crouched before a cold outside tap by a house nearly opposite mine.

I never gave much thought to why Māori lived in one area, and why their houses were often so poor. I suppose I took it for granted. But my complacency was shaken one evening, when I was watching a discussion about sporting contacts with South Africa, a regular feature on television. A New Zealand group named Halt All Racist Tours (HART) had just been established, intent on stopping the proposed 1969 All Black tour of that country which, they kept pointing out, was ruled by a racist regime under the segregationist policy called apartheid. The news footage from South Africa depicted the stark difference between white people's homes and the poor housing of black people.

It did not take much to recognise that a similar contrast could be seen in New Zealand and right outside my door in Carmichaels Road. It perplexed me that no one was drawing attention to this fact, on the television, in the newspapers or even in the conversations of adults. No one I knew spoke of the disparity in wealth and housing conditions that I saw around me, so maybe it did not matter; *maybe it did not even exist.* I remained troubled; the unspoken seemed unspeakable.

———

It was in the small Bethlehem shopping area that I had my first glimpse of what might lie behind these stark inequalities and tensions. When a shop closed down, an old map appeared temporarily in the bare window. It was an official-looking hand-drawn map, showing in red the straight line of my road, Carmichaels Road. On the northern, harbour, side of that road was written clearly in neat ink: 'Area returned to the Natives'. I never saw the map again, but the odd phrase stuck in my mind.

Much later, I learned about the history of the area.[4] The people of the local pā are hapū of the Ngāti Ranginui iwi. Like the Ngāti Awa people around Whakatāne where I had lived, the Ngāti Ranginui had thrived economically before the 1860s, sending food and other goods to Auckland. When Pākehā forces invaded the Waikato in 1863, Ngāti Ranginui sent fighters to help resist the British troops. The government also sent troops to Tauranga. In response, Ngāti Ranginui sent a letter to the British military camp asking, 'What is the meaning of the coming of the Englishmen to my place? ... Cease to come upon my piece of land.'[5] The officers took no heed: their forces not only killed the main leaders of Ngāti Ranginui, but the government confiscated almost 300,000 acres (120,000 hectares) of land, including the Bethlehem area. The New Zealand Settlements Act of 1863 had allowed the government to confiscate land from any tribes who resisted the Pākehā troops as they forcibly opened up land for settlement.

Small portions of the vast tracts of land taken in the raupatu (confiscation) were later returned to Māori, but often to individual owners rather than tribal communities, and particularly to those who did not resist the confiscation and land surveys. Carmichaels Road, no doubt marking a random delineation, sectioned off part of a strip of coastal land 'returned to the Natives' including hapū of Ngāti Ranginui.

Terrible hardship followed these government actions. In 1898, a Crown official described the people of the Bethlehem pā as having only enough land 'to starve on'. Even into the 1920s, many in the region were close to starvation, and a 1936 survey of Māori housing in the Tauranga area found one in three dwellings was 'unfit for human habitation'.[6]

This story, when I finally learned it, made sense of our experiences with our Māori neighbours in Bethlehem. These distressing events, still present in the recollections of parents and grandparents, had led to the poverty of the local Māori people and, by extension, my own relatively privileged position. This point would be made publicly in 2012 by the Waitangi Tribunal's finding that the unjust actions of the government in the 1860s caused 'significant harm to the [people's] social and economic development ... [a] burden carried by generations of Ngāti Ranginui ... which they continue to feel today'.[7] My house on the south side of Carmichaels Road was on confiscated land, and my family were beneficiaries of the Crown's enthusiastic immigration schemes that had flooded the land with white settlers, including my parents. The new immigrant families built their houses and developed their orchards and shops on what had, only a hundred years before, been Māori land. Although most Māori welcomed Pākehā technologies and laws in New Zealand, these laws were violently turned against the people – who would have shared the land, or otherwise negotiated a relationship with Pākehā coming to the district – leading directly to Māori poverty and hardship.

When I look back at the early-morning scene outside my gate in Carmichaels Road, I see it as alive with the flows of history and power that shaped all of our lives. Each of those acts of aloofness, flight, rage and anxiety amongst the children, as well as the mocking laughter, the clothes we wore, the food in our bags, the thoughts in our minds, and our positions in school – all these things were formed by the not-very-old story of the land where now wild paspalum grew, where rugby was played, and over which the bus packed with schoolchildren lumbered each day.

———

In my sixth-form year I became a prefect, and the next year, 1971, I was made Head Girl at Tauranga Girls' College. I was intensely ambivalent about my success. I wanted to be 'top of the school', but I also wanted to be released from the

Basil and Ruth Jones in 1952 on board the *Tamaroa*, bound for New Zealand.
In England, Basil had secured a job at the Bank of New Zealand in Auckland.
They were just married and excited about the new life ahead. *Alison Jones
collection*

My father, Basil, in Newcastle upon Tyne about 1942, in the lane where he grew up. Ten years later, to his parents' great dismay, he would migrate to the other side of the world with an unsuitable woman. Dad was entranced by the clean, open, wild landscapes of New Zealand. *Alison Jones collection*

My parents, Basil and Ruth, in Auckland in March 1953. Locals blamed newly arrived 'Poms' for 'taking our jobs'. My mother was happily pregnant, but my father was alarmed that they were starting a family so quickly after arriving.

Alison Jones collection

Above Through the winter of 1954, my mother pushed me in my comfortable English pram along Karangahape Road, Auckland. *Alison Jones collection*

Below A portrait taken in Blenheim in 1954, with my parents Ruth and Basil, and my new twin siblings. I am already responsible and anxious. *Alison Jones collection*

In a photograph taken when I was two years old, I clutch a hard-bodied doll. I am looking at the camera with a forced smile. I am wearing new shoes sent from England. *Alison Jones collection*

Above The family in Dannevirke. I am on the right in a new dress sent from my grandmother in England. Aged about nine, I am learning about a world outside my own. *Alison Jones collection*

Below A school portrait at Apanui Primary School in Whakatāne, 1965. A curious and diligent child, I was in my element in the classroom. *Alison Jones collection*

Above In 1968, my friend Jackie and I were confirmed in the Anglican Church. A photograph in the *Whakatane Beacon* showed us seated together, demure in virginal white. I am on Jackie's left. *Photograph by William Burgess for the* Whakatane Beacon, *20 November 1968*

Below Hilda Halkyard challenges the 'haka party', a group of engineering students at the University of Auckland in 1979. Who could fail to admire her courage? *Photograph by Iain Neill for* Craccum *magazine, vol 53, no.12, 5 June 1979, p.4*

broadsheet

NEW ZEALAND'S FEMINIST MAGAZINE

OCTOBER 1982 NO. 103 $1.80

Rebecca
Evans
on Her Life

Donna
Awatere
on Maori
Sovereignty

Bad news
in the
Budget

The scandal
of the
Children's
Homes

The cover of the feminist magazine *Broadsheet*. Prominent radical Māori women Donna Awatere and Ripeka Evans were photographed in dark clothing, with black boots, staunch shades and grim expressions. The effect was electrifying. *Photograph by Gil Hanly for* Broadsheet, *103 (October 1982), University of Auckland Libraries and Learning Services Te Tumu Herenga*

responsibilities of that position. I envied the Māori girls around
me who seemed to have much more fun than I did. I was held
tight by my uncertainties, expressed in physical terms: I not
only had mortifying acne, but I suffered blinding migraines, and
was an asthmatic. It was as if 'the tension, surprise, fear and
delight of … the full existence' lodged in my skin, my brain and
my lungs.

Ambivalence about my power and success came to a head
one morning at assembly. I was rescued by Rāhera, the Deputy
Head Girl. Nothing seemed to faze her. Without blushing, she
wore her grandfather's braces to hold up her rather too-large
regulation school skirt. She had a blazing confidence and sense
of humour.

All the pupils were required to enter the assembly hall at
8.45 a.m. in class rows to await the teachers' formal arrival
on the stage. That arrival was to be greeted with a respectful
silence, and it was my job as Head Girl to ensure such deference.
One morning, the girls would not settle down. Standing on the
stage, I insisted through the microphone that if they did not
become silent immediately I would call a 'practice assembly' at
lunchtime. My threat had such little effect that, after her arrival
on stage, Mrs Drayton, the principal – in the imposing academic
gown she wore to assemblies – had to sternly quieten the girls.
After assembly, I announced in my most imperious tone that
every girl must come back to the hall before they ate lunch.

Never was an instruction issued with more anxiety. I was
fully aware that if the girls disobeyed me, my power would
become a permanent joke. I would be humiliated. Surely the
students – especially the gutsy Māori girls – would resist? I
wanted to be a leader who was obeyed out of love and respect;
why should any of the students respect me? Was I simply a

minor tyrant? My mother had warned me about the female leader's sin: I was getting 'too big for my boots'. It was a stomach-churning morning; I distractedly recorded French verbs and physics equations in my textbooks without the usual attention.

When the bell rang for lunch, I hurried down to the hall and stood expectantly on the stage. To my astonishment, girls filed in and filled the hall. Rāhera was herding them. Almost weeping with relief, but suitably grave, I thanked them all for coming, asked them to obey my instructions in future, and dismissed them quickly. As I left the hall, privately vowing never to test my power again, a resentful Pākehā girl, staring hard at my face, sneered: 'I wouldn't come to school looking like *that*.' Having gathered her own small nub of power, she had hit back where it hurt. I blushed behind my offending acne, slunk off to the prefects' room, and slumped into the corner of an old couch, feeling sorry for myself. Rāhera laughed. 'Don't cry, mate! At least they came!' she said. I had to smile, and felt a rush of gratitude at her generous sense of humour – and, as I came to think about it later, her willingness to protect my mana. Decades later, Rāhera would become the lead negotiator for Ngāti Pūkenga's Treaty settlements.

———

In Tauranga, my mother made friends with Sylvia Ashton-Warner, the Pākehā writer and teacher. For ten years in the 1950s and '60s, Sylvia had lived in Carmichaels Road near where we were now, while her husband Keith Henderson was the beloved headmaster at what was then called Bethlehem Māori School. I had read and admired Sylvia's remarkable autobiographical books *Spinster* and *Teacher* – raw and unflinchingly honest stories about being a teacher in rural Māori communities. She loved the romance of teaching children but she was far too inventive, singular and unstable to abide the daily demands of a school. She was *interesting*, and I wanted to meet her.

My mother took me to see her one weekend afternoon, in 1974, at her new house in town. I hoped for an inspiring conversation about teaching, and about Bethlehem in the 1950s. Sylvia was a wild creative teacher and, more importantly, she wrote about herself as a wild creative teacher. While others were teaching 'Janet, John, come look and see the boats', she used original ideas to teach writing to Māori children, drawing on each child's most vivid experiences for their reading vocabulary. As she put it in *Teacher*:

> Puki, who comes from a clever family, and whose mother and father fight bitterly and physically and often, breaking out in the night and alarming the children who wake and scream (I've heard all this myself), after learning two words in six months burst into reading on Daddy, Mummy, Puki, fight, yell, hit, crack, frightened, broom.[8]

Sylvia's rebellion against an education system that 'wanted to organise me in sober pedestrianism' appealed to the sober pedestrian in me who ached for liberation.[9] Sylvia was able to see the world around her with astonishing clarity. She would have seen and named the poverty in Carmichaels Road; she would have said the unspeakable. Sylvia insisted that her friends called her Mere. My mother – unable or unwilling to pronounce Māori words correctly – called her Mary. Sylvia was impulsive, self-centred and glamorous. She used to ring my mother to insist she come around immediately because Sylvia needed a friend at that moment.

The afternoon we visited, Sylvia was withdrawn and rude, saying we could have 'ten minutes only' of her time. She barely spoke to us, so I admired her grand piano, her paint brushes and art equipment, her extensive bookshelf and her house's modern architecture. I left both stimulated and disappointed. Years later, after Sylvia had died, by chance I stayed in that same house. She haunted me in the night with her loud piano playing and her violent mood. I ordered her phantom to leave me alone and she withdrew. In the morning, I told the new home owner about the ghostly visitation. 'Yes, Sylvia is still around,' she laughed, though I found it more disconcerting than amusing.[10]

———

Despite my continuing curiosity about the Māori world, which seemed so close and yet so very far away, in my last year of school I turned away from complexity and towards certainty. I would avoid difficult political questions and unfathomable people. I decided that I would become a scientist. I had completed a seventh form (year 13) school project on pollution – a term relatively new in popular use – and was aware of the European and North American conservation movements: caring for nature had begun to take hold in the public imagination, and certainly in mine. Like many others, I had been moved by the famous photograph *Earthrise* taken from Apollo 8 as it orbited the moon. It was a stunning image of the shining blue Earth in an endless black universe, above the arid, pockmarked lunar landscape. The threat to our lovely planet was, for me, most immediately evident in Vietnam where the US military was spraying millions of gallons of herbicides and defoliants over forests and fields. On an idealistic mission to literally rescue the earth, I planned to become a soil scientist and travel to Vietnam to work. I would leave New Zealand's enigmatic problems and work on something solid and worthwhile, with easier answers, somewhere else.

My bookish Pākehā friend, Lesley, and I decided we would go to Massey University's rural campus in Palmerston North because of its beautiful trees and, for me, the availability of a soil science course. I would study for a Bachelor of Agricultural Science and she would study Arts. We had rooms in a campus hostel; the government, through a bursary system based on school achievement, would pay for our food and accommodation (which, together, came to $10 a week) and books. I bought a bus ticket to Palmerston North, packed a rucksack and, in February 1972, set off from Tauranga with Lesley for university life.

My sister cried at my departure (or perhaps she was envious of my escape). My mother was happy I had decided to continue studying, though my opting for science mystified her. My father had been sceptical, even negative, about my going to university: 'A waste of time for a girl,' he said, predictably. But my teachers and I just assumed university was the next step. What else would I do? My parents gave me $50 and waved goodbye.

I admit now that my choice of a university in a middle-sized New Zealand town was an act of secret cowardice. To be a biggish fish in a small pond, I avoided the cities of Auckland and Wellington with their complicated problems and clever people. I was simply pleased to be leaving home, and my uncomfortable family, at last.

Impossible love

I did not actually get to study soil science. That subject, I discovered, was for boys, and the boys in the BAgSci (Bachelor of Agricultural Science) programme wore white gumboots, check shirts and awkward grins. They avoided conversation, and had no idea about the soil pollution in Vietnam, or Rachel Carson's doomsday ecology book *Silent Spring*. They wanted to use the soil rather than save it. But I remained attracted by the apparent clarity and neutrality of science, so I decided to enrol for a BSc instead, and became a very minor expert in the mating behaviour of the mallard duck.

Being a woman in science was not much fun in the early 1970s. I was dismayed at the profusion of white men in white coats (one of whom tried to seduce me); discouraged by the dearth of women lecturers; and devastated when I was barred from applying for a coveted summer job overseeing a gannet colony at Cape Kidnappers simply because of my gender (they gave no other explanation). A friend and I boycotted classes, demanding that we debate the ethics of unquestioned procedures in our biology curriculum, including 'pithing frogs', which entailed bashing live frogs unconscious before poking a needle into their brains, and doing experiments on live chicken foetuses. I was criticised as an idealist, and told to 'go over to Arts and do Philosophy'. I did.

In Arts, I discovered the marvellous history of science. I

was forced to rethink my standard view of science completely. Rather than yearn for the clarity of scientific knowledge, I learned to embrace the beautiful logic of scientific uncertainty. I read Thomas Kuhn's *The Structure of Scientific Revolutions* and learned that scientific knowledge can be understood as a product of culture, history and politics – that is, it expresses what it becomes possible to know at a particular time in history – rather than simply an aggregation of careful objective discoveries devoid of context. In philosophy classes, we debated the nature – and even the possibility – of objectivity. We talked about how the language of science and the nature of reality relate to each other. It was exciting to consider that the limits of our language defined the limits of our knowledge. We grappled with questions that had no clear answers. I was giddy with the idea that human apprehension of the world is infinitely complicated.

All this intellectual work, this wrestling with complexity and uncertainty, would prepare me for the thorny questions of how Māori encountered the world, and how Māori language formed a quite different reality from the one I took for granted. But at this point I was still to encounter Māori knowledge or language in any depth and, as far as I was aware, there were few Māori students at Massey. One significant moment, however, stays in the memory. I was collecting mail from my pigeonhole in a public area and a crowd had gathered, alive with waves of laughter, jeers, and shouts. A wild-haired Māori man was caught up in a slanging match with a group of Pākehā male students. I stood, curious and slightly alarmed, at the back of the crowd, catching glimpses of the man as he moved in the agile manner of the kaikōrero, berating his audience, entertaining them, and goading them too.

The man, it turned out, was Te Ringa Mangu Nathan Mihaka, known everywhere as Dun Mihaka, who was fast becoming a prominent activist for Māori rights, and for the use of Māori language in the New Zealand courts. He was targeted by police for his colourful and controversial protest actions. At the time, he was on a tour of New Zealand universities to speak about the history of Māori land confiscations by Pākehā and to gather support for the campaign against sporting contact with South Africa. The incident that day stuck with me: his sheer bravery was impressive, and his ability to manipulate an audience was extraordinary. For the first time, I witnessed Māori oratory, and became aware of a raw Māori anger.

To meet the ideas of uncertainty and ineffability in my philosophy classes was one thing, but to confront them in real life was a challenge of a completely different order. Grappling with complexity requires an ability to step aside, at least for a moment, from one's quickest emotions of defensiveness and anxiety, and I was not yet light on my feet. I felt Mihaka's anger directly; I took his accusations of Pākehā racism and destructive colonisation personally. I felt as though I had no room to move, no clever response. I could be sceptical about science's claim to brute objectivity; I could be outraged at the patriarchal limits on women's lives; I could rail against generalised racism. These things allowed me access to a safe moral high ground. But whether I liked it or not, I was very differently positioned in New Zealand's history and in relation to Māori. I had an unnerving sense that Mihaka's accusations were correct, but I could not bear to be an object of Māori criticism.

In that moment, my pleasure at the challenge of complexity deserted me; I was a coward with regard to Māori fury. I turned

away from it because I had no idea how to face it. I had no idea I
could face it.

———

In November 1974, equipped with my new BSc degree, I headed
for Auckland, the Big Smoke, without a plan. I had barely
noticed what had been happening at home in Bethlehem, where
my brother and sister had left home, and my mother had set off
alone to travel in Europe leaving my father with his anxieties,
a freezer full of food, and the two youngest children, now
teenagers.

In Auckland, I moved into a cheap rented villa in Freemans
Bay, not far from Karangahape Road where as a toddler I had
first learned to walk. Over the decades since my birth, Māori
and Pacific working people had continued to live in this area
where the factories and heavy industries had been, and in
some case still were, located. By the time I moved back, these
industries were moving away, to cheaper land on the southern
and western outskirts of the city.

For the first time in my adult life I encountered the urban
poor at close quarters. The streets of Freemans Bay and
Ponsonby were lively with ball games, parties, bicycles, kids,
dogs and fights. Smoke from umu earth ovens drifted across
the suburb. Screaming pigs were killed in backyards. People
wore traditional wrap-around lavalava and went barefoot or in
jandals, and dressed up for church on Sundays.

The area was changing rapidly. Māori and Pacific tenants
and house owners were moving to new state houses in the
suburbs, following the work and looking for better accommodation. Pākehā students like me, young professionals, trade

unionists and artists were attracted to the area's grubby, animated, bohemian feel. A few of my Pākehā friends with carpentry skills and enough money for a deposit bought houses from owners who were pleased to rid themselves of the run-down dumps.

I was happy to be in the inner city, but not in the flea- and cockroach-ridden houses. Beds were not fashionable then, and mattresses on the floor were the perfect territory for fleas. There came a night in the Freemans Bay flat when I turned back my sheets and recognised defeat: the crowd of jumping black insects were too much for me. Within a month, flea-bitten and sleep-deprived, I packed my possessions in my rucksack, and fled. I found a room in my boyfriend's Devonport flat where young architects, engineers, photographers and film-makers ate nuts and brown rice and grew their own vegetables. Although New Zealand was in an economic recession, with high unemployment and inflation, those who were employed felt optimistic, and rich as kings.

The Devonport group was inspired by the North American counterculture ideals of living simply off the land and sharing resources, and we soon grabbed an opportunity to live on rural land. Under the name Earth Extract, we leased hilly scrub land north of Auckland near Waipū, joining an idealistic Labour government programme called the Ohu scheme to house young people on rural land. Matiu Rata, the Minister of Lands, said that he hoped the Ohu scheme would 'lead the way to a more concerned society and recapture anew the deep links of people and land ... [and] the satisfaction based on co-operation, mutual assistance and communalism, which had been the force which motivated both the first Māori and the first European settlers of this land'.[1]

Some of the group moved to the land to build plywood houses and plant gardens; others, like me, stayed in Devonport, hitchhiking to the land on the weekends.

By now, my distance from the Māori world was such that two major shifts in modern Māori history in 1975 passed by like slow-moving scenes in the background. I was aware of them, but only from a distance. A massive hīkoi or march from the Far North of New Zealand to Parliament in Wellington to protest against Māori land loss had shocked many New Zealanders into knowledge about our shameful history of Māori land alienation. And a seismic shift in Māori access to legal remedy for these wrongs had finally taken place. The establishment of the Waitangi Tribunal (a permanent commission of inquiry, but not a court that could make enforceable judgments) provided a legal process for the investigation of Māori land grievances.

I was happily sleepwalking with no real desire to wake up to the world around me. I was focused on my own life, and what to do next. Since cutting my moorings to a career in science, I had been rudderless. And a few weekends at the ohu cutting mānuka scrub in the rain, trying to protect the vegetable garden from voracious possums, and cooking over a sputtering fire, put me off a life on the land. On a whim, I visited the imposing brick building of the nearby Takapuna Grammar School, knocked on the principal's door and asked if he had any jobs.

He did, as it happened. It was possible to teach without a teaching certificate in those days and I would be a relieving science teacher for the rest of the year while the regular teacher was on maternity leave. Earning decent money for the first time was a pleasurable shock, and I enjoyed my students. But I hated the petty school rules requiring me to confiscate jewellery, to invigilate hairstyles, and to formally witness vicious canings. On Friday afternoons, I read war stories to my lowest fourth form instead of vainly trying to teach them science; these were the Pākehā sons of parents working at the Devonport naval yards.

At the end of that year, I had saved enough money to travel somewhere. I did not have the funds for an airline ticket to England, where most young New Zealanders went for what would be called their Big OE, Overseas Experience. The only person I knew overseas was Malcolm, a young fisheries scientist based in Nukuʻalofa, Tonga. I could afford the plane ticket. I had few clues where Tonga was, except 'in the Pacific'. But I went anyway.

———

My few weeks in Tonga at the start of 1976 turned out to be less a holiday than a string of recalibrations of my cultural stereotypes. I recall my vague thoughts in the plane above the vast blue ocean. I imagined the romantic lives of the Pacific people. They ate from the land and sea, made picturesque houses of coconut palm, owned little and sang a lot. We Europeans were busy accumulating stuff and destroying the planet; we could learn a thing or two from the simple lives of the Pacific people, I thought.

I was enchanted by Tonga, and naïvely opinionated. When I remonstrated with a young man with a colourful tupenu around his waist about the new house he was building with cement block, corrugated iron and louvre windows, he fired back, 'What do you want here, lady? A museum?' His uncle had worked hard in New Zealand to send money to Tonga for the materials. I preferred the thatched fale, huts made entirely of woven coconut leaves, wood and fibre. The fale, I said, was more attractive and environmentally sound. He seemed annoyed at my ignorance. The concrete house is the best, I was told by others. Fale are easily damaged in high winds, insects live in the thatch, and they have to be regularly maintained. Only poor people live in them.

In the same village, I played in the sun with a baby boy named Koloni. His grandmother put her forefinger and thumb around my wrist and raised it for inspection. 'Ke fu'u pakau!' she harrumphed. 'Too thin! No wonder you are not married!' Koloni's mother, who had at least six other children, sat nearby in a short-sleeved shirt and a cotton tupenu, unpicking a plastic flour bag whose narrow strands would be used to crochet a ta'ovala, the woven waist mat worn on formal Tongan occasions. Koloni was chubby and bold, happy to sit on my legs, reaching for my fair hair and giggling at my game of 'boo!' As I cuddled and admired him, his mother spoke suddenly and intensely: 'You have him.' I looked up sharply, surely misunderstanding her words. 'You have him,' she repeated seriously. She wanted me to adopt her child. I stopped breathing, momentarily wondering whether I should accept her offer, but I quickly pushed away the idea with an embarrassed refusal: 'He would miss his mama!' I knew this was a poor reply to a mother with too many children and too few resources, whose baby could be the currency for a family entry ticket to a better life.

In Tonga, my pale skin alone marked me out as wealthy and privileged. Absurdly, I aspired to simply blend in, to become a benign observer of village life, but as a palangi I came with a history – whether I liked it or not. I came with all the baggage of European 'superiority' that had been at work in Pacific societies for the two hundred years since the arrival of mis-

sionaries. It was impossible for me to avoid Tongan deference.
In the crowded post office, I was always served before those
in front of me; at a funeral, I was asked to take an honoured
position near the front of the traditional procession through a
village, carrying a woven basket of faikakai (sweet dumplings);
I was extravagantly singled out for a welcome from the pulpit
during church services; I was sought out as a server for kava
ceremonies. Toddlers reared away from me with parents'
warnings that 'the palangi will get you'. Any resistance towards
such moments of respect, adulation or fear would offend.
Behaving in a culturally appropriate manner, I began to see, was
a complicated matter.

These complexities were everywhere. Travelling around
Tonga, I encountered a delightful array of animals, but they
were often treated badly. Pigs, and sometimes dogs, were
bashed to death or hideously injured with sticks or coconuts;
live turtles and big coconut crabs were tied up and poked to
death by children. Men lay and chatted in the shade while old
women carried bundles of firewood; children with folded arms
sat on concrete classroom floors inside small painted squares
watching for the teacher's stick; preachers in remote churches
shouted about hellfire and damnation; all my underpants were
taken by village girls, who had none; white American volunteer
workers were respected while an African American volunteer
was disdained for her dark skin colour.

I struggled with these disturbing events in otherwise
intensely happy days. My travelling companion was a Tongan-
speaking American boyfriend I acquired in Nuku'alofa, whose
presence was legitimised by a fake wedding ring. Ordinary
village people welcomed me and my 'husband' with an insistent
pleasure. We lived amongst people whose lives had changed

little over two hundred years. I sat on the ground with the gossiping women, grating coconuts on old iron implements, and cooking fresh fish in banana leaves in earth ovens. I listened to stories, sometimes translated by my companion. One I remember was about how men fishing for shark would once toss freshly cooked pork and flowers into the sea from their boat, calling a secret poem to the shark. If an approaching shark looked dark, it was angry, so the men apologised and left it alone. If the shark was lighter in colour, it would be able to be roped and lifted in to the boat to be killed with a club blow. I could listen to these tales over and over again, even in a language I could barely comprehend. I simply enjoyed the animation of the speaker, and the pleasure of the listeners sitting close around a fire, or on the sandy beach where huge hairy pigs dug with their snouts for cockles, and the sun faded across the ocean.

I wholeheartedly loved the women who, fully clothed, sat in the sea in the hot late afternoon talking and laughing. My bones vibrated to the hard, bright sound of the village hymns, and melted at the children's singing as they played. Children on the beach on the little island of 'Ofu in Vava'u, taught me the Tongan version of the nursery rhyme 'Pussy cat pussy cat where have you been?': Ki'i pusi, ki'i pusi-i / Na'a ke 'i fe ai pe he aho ni? / Na'a ku 'alu ki Lonitoni / 'O 'a 'ahi ki he Kuini. I showed villagers my fold-out paper map, pointing to where Tonga was a mere dot in the huge blue ocean, and Lonitoni – London – was near the top of the world. My supply of Dettol disinfectant, which I applied to the kids' and adults' sores on the remote island of Niuatoputapu, improved the social status of my host family's village as well as their health. My elastoplasts decorated proud children's arms. In these moments, perhaps revelling in the age-old power of the rich Western traveller, perhaps feeling genuinely *useful* for once, I felt brightly happy.

And yet ... I was exhausted by the sheer *foreignness* of the place. Men pestered me with their quick eyebrows even though I was 'married'. Myriad rules governed my every action: no work of any sort (even unpicking a sack for its thread) was to be done on Sundays; Tongan clothes were to be worn to church, where we went several times a week; women were always to sit at the back at public events. Meanwhile, the lack of privacy and the unstinting curiosity about the strange palangi wore me down. My cultural need for solitude almost overwhelmed me. I was offered a job as a teacher in a remote village. Fakamolemole, I said – sorry, I want to go home.

I had no career plan, but neither did I want to travel on to England as some of my friends had done. The land of my parents felt almost as far away from me as it was from my little teachers, the happy children who sang 'Ki'i pusi, ki'i pusi-i'. My first overseas trip had not turned my gaze outward; rather I was drawn into a deeper sense of my own place *here* in the Pacific.

———

Back in Auckland in the early autumn of 1976, I needed a job. I found a temporary teaching position at Bollard Girls' Home in Avondale, Auckland, which was, in effect, a prison for adolescent girls. A vivid memory from my first day is being issued with a heavy bunch of keys. I was incredulous and almost laughed: I had only seen such keys on television cop shows.

A two-room school was on site. The other teacher was a Pākehā woman who had fostered dozens of Māori and Pacific children. She was a trained Anglican minister, and she spoke

Māori and Samoan. I remember her as warm, with a wide bosom on which lay a wooden crucifix that hung from her neck. She had a kind, cheerful face. She believed in evil spirits, and that some of the girls were subject to bad forces. I did not question her viewpoint – I was, after all, a newcomer – and I could see that the girls loved her. She was, in the best possible way, in the rescue business; I was, initially anyway, doing a paid job, being kind to girls whose lives I could barely imagine.

Almost all of the girls at Bollard Girls' Home were Māori, aged between about thirteen and fifteen. Police or social workers had collected some of them off the Auckland streets as runaways or sex workers, or for 'not being in the control of a responsible adult'. Others had been taken from their homes to escape domestic violence, sexual abuse or parental neglect. Girls came and went from the institution and my classroom. I devised individual writing and reading programmes, building on what they already knew. Some were advanced; others were slow. Within a few days or weeks they were sent to relatives or foster families, other institutions or, sometimes, back home.

I adored those girls with a fierce, motherly love. They were funny, intelligent and tough. I believed that if I loved them enough, they would love me back. Sometimes, they did, hugging me roughly as though I were a large rag doll. With my attention and affection, I thought, I could protect them. My own needs were part of it: beyond the naïve optimism that my love would save them, I was looking for some sort of redemption. Their love would signal that I was special, a helper, not a hinderer. Their love would somehow liberate me from the harsh history that shaped their lives.

What I did not quite realise then was that I was not special; no one is. We are all born into a family history and its place in the social order. Our birth circumstances, like rivers, pull each of us along in their own tides and flows. I was held in an external current that inevitably carried me along, like an Old Testament whakapapa: the colonisation of New Zealand begat my English parents' immigration to New Zealand middle-class life, which begat cultural rewards, which begat my going to university, which begat teaching there at that moment. For the Bollard girls, the path from colonisation flowed so differently, from ancestral land loss (or in the case of Pacific girls, an immigrant journey that delivered them into the New Zealand working class) to urbanisation to family poverty to incarceration. Our presence in that small, warm classroom, which I had decorated with pictures of beautiful exotic animals, boiled down, in its simplest terms, to a series of historical currents that entangled my life with theirs.

My naïve beliefs did not mean that, for those girls, love was a reliable refuge. My implicit request that they be open to my love invited a suspicious, resentful response. Sheryl, who was fourteen, had been at a succession of schools. I spent time with her, gently coaxing her to write. Then one winter's afternoon, in the quiet classroom, Sheryl picked up a heavy old typewriter and threw it at me. I dodged, and the machine crashed to the floor. Sheryl was not allowed back at the school after that. Other days, with other girls, a chair or a pair of scissors became a defensive weapon holding my affection at bay; I was lucky not to be injured. It took days to convince the home's manager to allow me to take eleven-year-old Karlene out for a weekend treat. The youngest girl at Bollard, Karlene vowed solemnly she would not abscond from my care. When she jumped out of the car at the first traffic lights without saying a word, all I could do was weep with frustrated confusion. She had been focused from the outset on escaping from the institution back to her (violent) family.

Recaptured by the police, Karlene was locked in a punishment room that, ironically, went by the name 'secure'. 'Secure' was modelled on real prison conditions: there were bars on the single, high window, a rubber-covered mattress, a metal seatless toilet. The prison experience was supposed to scare Karlene into behaving herself. But she just lay on the mattress on the floor and chewed a hole in the regulation grey blanket. I took her a polyanthus plant, and a book. It was unbearable, seeing her in that bare viewless room. Later, we exchanged a few letters. She told me she was looking after the plant, which now had flowers coming up from it. She said 'the book you gave me is a good book' and apologised for not writing often. She always ended her letters with 'Lots of love Karlene xxxxxx'.

Wanting, impossibly, to form a relationship with the girls, I responded openly to their insatiable curiosity about me: where did I live, what were my parents like, who was my boyfriend and why did I like him? What did we do on the weekends and in the holidays? Some wrote me cheerful letters after they left, recalling our fun times, missing the other girls, reassuring me they would not be back in Bollard, wishing me and my family a Happy Christmas. I couldn't help worrying when Sharly proudly reported she had a 'big tough fella' boyfriend named Kaos.

On Friday nights, ex-Bollard girls – and soon-to-be Bollard girls – hung about outside Mojo's, a city nightclub famous for its floor show featuring drag queens, many of whom were Māori. On the pavement, Māori and Pacific youths would gather to catch up with each other, and to eyeball the police who habitually parked nearby. Any kid who swore or gestured obscenely at 'the pigs' would be handcuffed and manhandled into one of the police vehicles while the others booed and jeered, and passers-by hurried on. I witnessed this performance more than once; it was electrifying. The police played their role as keenly as the hostile crowd: the kids demonstrated their bravado, and the same scene played out week after week. Young Māori and Pacific girls would get their few minutes of fame being dragged into a police car, and end up back in Bollard. I had ready judgments, and I was on the side of the girls. I could not work out why the police loitered on this part of the street, not only waiting for trouble but, by their presence, actively provoking it. As for the girls, I had learned enough to know they had nothing much to lose by being taken back to Bollard; it was sometimes preferable to the alternative.

What troubled me most was the ethnicity of the differenti-ated groups in the Friday-night pantomime: Māori and Pacific kids jeering at the police, Pākehā police waiting to be offended, and displeased Pākehā passers-by watching 'bad kids' and 'police doing their job'. I, too, was a Pākehā onlooker. No doubt the girls wondered why I was there (I had come to say hello to them). It did not occur to me to intervene, to question the police about their provocations.

———

I had already had the experience of being a witness out of place – in an adult prison, about three years before I worked at Bollard. It was the early 1970s and my friends and I, galvanised by North American social liberation movements, were energised by outrage about social inequality. I wanted to do something *practical*. I had signed up for prison visiting over the summer of 1973–74, between semesters away at Massey University. The programme was operated out of the run-down Progressive Youth Movement (PYM) offices in Ponsonby Road in Auckland, to help families visit their men in Mt Eden jail – a place that looked like a medieval dungeon, and was originally a military stockade, built in 1857 to hold the armaments used against Māori. Now, Māori men were the majority of the inmates. The PYM wanted volunteers for prisoners who had no visitors. My name and address were passed to a prisoner, who replied with the required visitors' slip, and a note in impeccably neat, sloping italics saying : 'Thank you, for being able to pay, yours truly, a visit ... that's really cool of you.'

Akarana was a handsome and charming man doing a long sentence for repeated serious crimes. Throughout the summer, I visited him weekly and we talked – about philosophy, morality, spirituality and freedom. 'Everyone is in their own prison', he said, 'even you. This is mine.' He recommended the teachings of Krishnamurti, the then-popular Indian spiritual philosopher who taught that freedom is a state of mind.

From time to time he also wrote me articulate letters, elaborately decorated in the margins with flowers and fancy lettering, and filled with loosely connected thoughts and witty observations about prison life. Then he began to talk about 'us' as though we had a shared future. I was out of my depth, and horrified at my naïvety: what else did I expect to happen when a young woman gave attention to a lonely man? I made up an excuse and stopped going to the jail.

I still sometimes think about my visits to the prison, and how my rescue fantasies made me feel good about 'doing something'. Just as I had wanted to rescue the Tongan baby Koloni from his family's poverty and the Bollard girls from their difficult lives, I wanted to redeem Akarana, but they only existed for me – really – in the abstract. My life fleetingly intersected with theirs, and to do any more than express kindness seemed impossible. We were all caught in the great structural inequalities from which I benefited, and they did not. I was far enough outside their lives to step quickly away.

My prison visits allowed me many glimpses into other worlds. One day in the visiting hall, I noticed a straight-backed man leaning in concentration towards his two visitors. The quiet intensity of the seated trio seemed to suck the air from the room. Such was the man's dignity and bearing, he put me in mind of a king or noble warrior who overwhelm by their sheer presence. I had never had this feeling before; it shook me, and I wondered who this man could be.

I found out that he was Arapeta Marukitepua Pitapitanuia-rangi Awatere, whom I had heard of as Colonel Awatere. He was a member of the fabled 28th (Māori) Battalion in the Second World War – indeed, he had briefly led it, in Italy, and he had been an Auckland city councillor for much of the 1960s. He was trained in karakia, whaikōrero and whakapapa, and the history and use of ancient weapons. His visitors that day – intense and absorbed in their encounter – were his daughter Donna and her then boyfriend Norman. Awatere had been convicted of murder, and imprisoned for killing his mistress's lover. Donna would later write that at their prison meetings, her father was educating her: 'The thing he talks about most is the Treaty of Waitangi and what's happening to our people. It was when I was [visiting him] in prison that the responsibility he felt he carried for his people was passed to me.' [2]

Sometimes, a small fleeting experience can have a profound effect. On this day, just seeing Colonel Awatere's face shifted my perspective. In this hard, high-ceilinged, rock-walled room, Awatere's striking presence alerted me again to knowledges and histories outside my awareness. I held my breath. An endless space opened: my ignorance, hitherto largely invisible to me, seemed suddenly limitless. The universe expanded as I sensed – inchoately, vaguely, uncertainly – a deep, wide, Māori world. Its landscapes, unnamed, unthought, unknowable by me, were there. *Here*.

———

I looked for summer work. I applied to a spring-making factory in Kingsland, where the boss, a chubby and cheerful Pākehā man, showed me through the dirty old Dickensian wooden building above the new north-western motorway. Young and old Pacific women worked at roaring machines that clanked and thundered so loudly conversation was impossible. The room was dangerous and dark. With the privilege of other options, I fled, horrified at work conditions I had never seen before. I waitressed in the evenings at Tony's Restaurant in Wellesley Street, where the only irritations were smirking male cooks who forced me to press up against them as I passed through the narrow kitchen with dirty dishes.

I really cannot remember if I thought much about Māori as such in those days. I check my old diaries, endless boringly self-obsessed pages of angst about my sexual relationships, and find the odd remark. I seem to look at Māori 'out there' with a sense of distance, slight superiority and unease.

Monday May 10th 1976

Waiting for the ferry, Steve and I eat in a scruffy cafeteria at the Wellington Railway Station: milkshake, sandwiches, pie, cake. All Island or Maori girls, with lovely smooth skin, behind the counters, cheerful, boisterous. Walked to the terminal choking in the grime and fumes of the working wharves. We passed the railway workers: rough men and boys, most brown faces, fat singlet-ed bellies. These men feed the nation. Even so, I recoil from that grimy existence. How those grubby men must dislike us: clean, disdainful of them.

———

Towards the end of the next summer, on a whim, I tagged along for a visit with a Pākehā friend who knew a lecturer who happened to teach philosophy of education at the University of Auckland. Just because I had nothing better to do, and 'the philosophy of' *anything* appealed to me, I ended up enrolling in 1977 for a postgraduate degree in Education. I reasoned that I did not like school teaching, but at least education is socially useful. It would postpone the necessity of planning my life.

Some decisions seem easy only because they encounter no resistance. The garden outside the lecturer's office was brightly pretty, the lecturer was welcoming and handsome, and on the office verandah a fantail darted eagerly at spiders. I did not know I was entering an academic pathway and a close relationship with Māori from which I would not emerge.

Middle-class olives, and revolution

One day in May 1978, I was in the university library, at my customary study spot near the catalogue cabinets on the ground floor. It was peaceful – libraries were in those days – when, with a sudden crash, the main doors burst open. About seven young men, their faces and naked chests smeared with what looked like brown shoe polish and lipstick, raffia grass skirts over their shorts, raced inside. Two leapt on the catalogue cabinets, banging at their chests, poking out their tongues, gabbling and shouting. One loudly bashed a drum. They raced up the library stairs, hooting as they went.

I had heard of this 'haka party': a few Pākehā engineering students ran around the campus each year during capping week, doing so-called war dances. Māori had for twenty years condemned this insult to the haka and written to the group asking them to desist. One of their chants was reported to be 'Ka mate! Ka mate!' (stamping feet and slapping thighs), 'Hori! Hori!' (left hand patting head, right hand simulating masturbation), 'I got the pox from Hori! Hori!'[1] Some wrote obscenities and drew sexual organs on their bodies. Like most other students, I thought their actions were pathetic – childish and plain dumb. Once they had crashed their way out of the library, my fellow readers and I simply turned back to our studies, resentfully tolerating their woeful antics, as we might any drunken reveller.

It was to be the haka party's swansong. The following year, a
Māori activist group called He Taua (the war party) confronted
the engineering students as they rehearsed their stunt at
the School of Engineering. A fight broke out. Some students
were hospitalised, and the activists were charged with assault.
The press condemned what it called Māori 'gang violence'. As
Ranginui Walker put it: 'A fracas ensued, the students were
assaulted, and their grass skirts torn from them. In less than
five minutes of direct action, the gross insult of the haka party
was stopped where years of negotiation failed.'[2]

———

My brother and I fell out badly over this incident. He was at the
engineering school at the time, though not a member of the
haka party. He took the view – as many others did – that the
mock haka was 'only a bit of fun', that oversensitive liberals
like me were making mountains out of molehills, and the
Māori 'gang' who beat up the students were violent thugs. My
opposing position was probably as uninformed as my brother's.
I reflexively cheered for anyone who dared challenge these
engineering oafs but I was moderate in my support of the
challengers. In a letter to a friend in May 1979 I wrote: 'I heard
that the haka party morons got beaten up. The Maoris went a
bit far with the violence. I think I am a pacifist. I bet it worked
though!'

When I discussed this event with my parents later, they
thought the beating was 'a bit unnecessary'. They both
concluded their opinions with the comment 'but I know nothing
about it', which closed down any further conversation. For
them, ignorance was equivalent to innocence, an honourable

refuge, and the basis of an even-handed and honest view. The statement 'I don't know enough about it, and I want to stay out of it' provided an imagined moral high ground, above complex political questions. Ignorance was a useful debate-stopper, and my father disliked argument.

My own ignorance was probably strong, too. But admitting that I didn't know enough was not an option. I always had an opinion, even if it was based on little information. What I lacked in knowledge I made up for with instinct. I was beginning to grasp the theoretical concept of power and other big ideas encountered at university, like structural inequality and oppression. Here were ideas to think with, intellectual frameworks that made sense of my instincts, that fuelled a burning desire to *do something* – to counter oppression, to right wrongs, to make a difference – rather than just to observe.

'Making a difference' meant protesting. With many other young students, I was caught up in a flurry of exciting but exhausting and sometimes dangerous activities. It is hard to explain to young people now how intense and constant was the political action in Auckland in the late 1970s and early 1980s. I joined activist groups of Pākehā fired up about injustice. Change seemed possible and necessary. We joined marches for abortion and home birth, against rape, poverty and nuclear weapons. We wore the bruises from police batons or fists proudly, our badges of honour. Some of us set up soup kitchens in public parks to draw attention to poverty in the city. Some women put quick-setting cement down toilets of what they claimed were sexist organisations. My friends and I drove around Auckland at night in an old van full of screen-printed posters and buckets of glue, dashing out at intervals to slap up our anti-capitalist or anti-royalist messages on city buildings.

I was one of a group of women who roped off the busiest inter-
section in the city to disrupt traffic and gain media attention
about access to abortion. I felt both terrified and elated to be
sitting and chanting in the middle of the main street, full of
youthful excitement and possibility. I joined, and led, feminist
consciousness-raising groups and a health centre for women.[3]
My most intrepid action was lobbing paint-filled eggs at sexist
advertising billboards from the back of a friend's motorbike, in
the dead of night. Although I felt very daring, when I missed the
billboard I couldn't help worrying about the mess I had made.

There were so many protest possibilities, and that variety
brought its own challenges. The old mass social movement of
socialism was fracturing into many smaller protest movements.
The ideals of difference and diversity had displaced workers'
solidarity – such solidarity, for our generation, merely masked
a lot of competing interests. We quickly became issues-based
in our protests, fired up by protest movements in the United
States, Australia and Britain. We were 'pro-choice' and helped
women get abortions in Australia; we railed against the
patriarchy's subjugation of women, discrimination against
homosexuals and lesbians, the power of capitalists and
oppression of the workers; we demanded an end to nuclear
weapons testing and collected signatures for the huge 1976
petition for a nuclear-free New Zealand; we opposed apartheid
in South Africa, sided with the Black Liberation movement in
the US, and read about the fate of Native American people.

I relished the hours I spent at the art gallery coffee bar, and
in the university quad, arguing about the meaning of classism
or how power worked. Our overarching analysis was clear and
simple, and power was at the centre of it: some groups had
more power that allowed their interests to be met over those

of others. In particular, sexism, racism and classism formed the rules and attitudes that kept men, white people and middle-class people in power. For us, the land was populated with goodies and baddies – respectively with more, or less, power over the conditions of our lives. That ancient, satisfying dualism simplified our thinking and fired our protest actions.

I found discussions with feminist friends most satisfying, and spent less and less time with male activists. Most of the men I knew seemed to be frightened of feminism, and of feminists, and the day one of my male friends made a disparaging remark about my (politically) hairy legs was the last day I bothered talking politics with men – for a while, at least.

On the ground amongst the women, a fierce identity politics was developing. In simple terms, we feminists identified ourselves as women battling against the power of the patriarchy. But being a woman was complicated. That identity was immediately cross-cut with other identities: lesbian, heterosexual, radical, liberal, woman-of-colour, working class, Jewish, and so on. With our simple binary analyses of power, we each found ourselves multiply positioned on the good/bad identity divide: I was (am) a heterosexual (bad), white (bad), middle-class (bad) woman (good). Many of my friends were lesbian, and I was under some pressure to join them. I did think about it. 'Sorry,' I apologised, half in jest. 'I can't help being straight!' I wrote an article titled 'Sleeping with the enemy'.

Things reached a crisis at a Women's Liberation Congress held at Piha on Auckland's west coast in early 1978. Some of the participants criticised the organisers as 'alienating' and 'middle-class' for serving black olives at lunch. Then there was the attempt by some self-proclaimed radical feminists to expel members of the Socialist Action League from the conference because they gave their allegiance to a male political party. Lesbians refused to caucus with women they cursed as 'hets'. Sisterhood was, as some of us noted later, clearly savage and unsentimental stuff.[4]

An unsatisfying solution to all this complexity was the idea that all women are oppressed, though some are more oppressed than others. Positioning oneself on this hierarchy of oppression became ritualised to the extent that at meetings, women intoned their personal identity in terms of political categories. At a Socialism Meets Feminism conference, a workshop on socialist economics began with all the women taking turns to identify themselves. The workshop convenor made it clear what was expected with 'I am a middle-class lesbian Jew, an academic with white privilege.' The prouder end of the hierarchy of oppression was represented by 'I am a working-class dyke active in the trade-union movement.'[5] I had rather too many privileges to mention, and I resentfully rebelled. 'I am Alison,' I said. 'I am a student at the University of Auckland.'

I was more than a little sceptical about these identity wars because they conceived of power as being primarily possessed by individuals. As a middle-class woman, I had more power than a working-class woman, for instance. It was implied that my power was like a pile of biscuits I could redistribute to my poorer sisters. (In fact, I heard there was a workshop where people were given a number of actual vanilla wine biscuits commensurate with their social power, and they had to give them away to people with fewer.) Of course, I believed in a radical redistribution of wealth, but to think I could 'give away my power' seemed both wrong-headed and impossible. One aspect of 'sharing power' in our meetings involved going around the room inviting every single woman to speak, even if all she said was: 'I'm only here to listen' or 'I just want to be here in support.' This pointless 'sharing' sometimes went on for hours, and I was beside myself with frustration. I went back to my student flat after meetings with a sharp stomach ache and a grim expression. Politics was not much fun at all, but I was compelled to do *something* and was unsure what else to do.

My stress compounded when we tried collectively to write down our ideas. I was part of a group formed to produce a newspaper named *Bitches, Witches and Dykes – A Women's Liberation Newspaper*. Our editorial in Volume One, Number One, August 1980 was headed in thundering capital letters TOWARDS REVOLUTION. We laid out the nature of the task before us with a naïve and idealistic grandiosity: 'Equality with men inside the established society will not change patriarchal, capitalist, heterosexist and white supremacist culture. We therefore see that our goal is a feminist revolutionary process that changes the entire social order.'[6]

We were deadly serious, arguing long and hard over virtually each word we wrote. I can hear my scepticism in this conversation, recorded by one of our group as we produced the editorial.

Alison: What about this sentence? It sounds ungrammatical.

B: I don't think so.

C: It's contradictory.

D: It is not.

Alison: It sounds like rhetoric to me, jargon.

B: Well, it is jargon, but it's hard to avoid some times.

Alison: Well, I don't like it. You've got 'patriarchal, capitalist, heterosexist, white, male supremacist'. It's too much.

C: What about racist, you haven't got racist.

B: Yes, I have. White male supremacist equals racist.

Alison: The whole thing is too woolly. We've got to tighten it up.

D: No, I like it the way it is …[7]

In an attempt to cheer myself up, I wore builders' overalls that I had dyed pink, and usually decorated them with a political badge or two: *Abortion: A Woman's Right to Choose*, or *Fight Inequality!* I rode a Suzuki motorbike and enjoyed the freedom of riding fast, and 'passing' as a man in my helmet, boots and jacket.

As anti-white-supremacy activists, it was obvious that we needed to involve Māori women in the newspaper. I took a breath and rang Ripeka Evans. I was jokingly self-deprecating without being too pathetic: 'We're "anti-racist" these days, us Pākehā, you know, Rebecca [as she was known then]. So help! We need you!' It seemed faintly embarrassing, but Ripeka was warm – yes, she would write something, and so would some of her friends. 'But you know the drill, we'll need editorial autonomy!' She said this wryly, as though we both knew the political game we were playing together. She made me laugh. 'In fact, it will have to be a whole separate paper,' she added. We agreed that her paper would be inside ours, like a pull-out. We would pay for the layout, publishing and printing costs. She made it sound as though she was doing us a favour, which, I suppose, she was.

Ripeka called the section *Black Forum*. Taking up the inspirational rhetoric of the Black Liberation Movement in North America, and anti-racism discourses, Māori radicals were teaming up with Pacific Islands activists as Blacks. She called for Black women to unite: 'We have come together as Black Women, Māori, Pacific Island and other Black women to fight whites in Aotearoa who are exploiting our labour to increase their own white wealth.'[8]

My being white never seemed to bother Ripeka, who was a confident woman intent on political change for Māori. She welcomed allies and relationships that helped her own political plans. She had been to Cuba to study leftist politics, and as a result was reportedly on a government terrorist watch-list. Everyone was suitably impressed. As we worked together, Ripeka and I learned that we shared a sense of unease in our respective political work. Neither of us was very happy – we both suffered from a sense of depression, and in her words saw ourselves as 'optimistic pessimists'. We both felt the demand for conformity to certain group analyses based on femaleness and, ultimately, whiteness. Ripeka indicated that she also thought it was all too intense – the petty arguments and constant demands to have opinions exhausted both of us. She confessed that being a Māori activist leader was complex: 'We have to be all things to all people,' she said, 'we have to have all the answers, always be consistent, and we are always criticised anyway.' It surprised me to learn that she, too, wanted at times to step outside the constant noise and action, just as I did, to go somewhere quiet and simply have liberated time.

———

Neither *Bitches, Witches and Dykes* nor the *Black Forum* lasted long. Their fates were intertwined. The editorial of the fourth and final issue noted the collective's demise. It was titled 'From the collective (without consensus)', and identified the problem: our racism. 'As we started to develop what would become *BWD* we wanted to see ourselves as having an anti-racist perspective. We soon found that *wanting* to have an anti-racist perspective, and *having* one, were two different things,' the editorial began. Apparently, Ngahuia Te Awekotuku, a well-known Māori feminist activist, had sent a letter to the collective for publication 'charging us all with racism and questioning our policies on the Black Women's Forum'.[9] The editorial neglects to explain the content of the letter. I do not remember it, though I assume it was about the separation of the *Black Forum* section of the paper and its otherwise 'white orientation' when it was supposed to be about 'women's liberation'.

Some other Black women had approached the collective to ask that the letter not be published. This caused a heated discussion in our group about censorship. Were we, a group of white women, to censor a letter sent to us by a Black woman, because other Black women had asked us to? On the one hand, we (bizarrely) blamed ourselves for racism for being unable to discuss the matter without a meltdown, and on the other, we blamed Ngahuia for trying 'to force us to be the arbiters of Black issues'. This interesting complexity seemed to be the beginning of the end for us, and my suspicions about the poor analytic value of the weapon-term 'racism' were reinforced.

———

Finding feminist politics stressful and inward-looking, I was drawn to the left-wing Republicans, led by the low-key and brilliant Pākehā couple Bruce and Joce Jesson. The Republicans' aim was an independent New Zealand socialist economy. I regularly spent time at their Ōtāhuhu home, listening to the discussions and helping to print and mail out *The Republican* magazine, a leading radical political newsletter of the time. A question discussed in its pages was whether there could be a radical alliance between the Pākehā left and Māori radicals. The general consensus from the Pākehā Republican left seemed to be positive.[10]

I was the kind of Republican Bruce found mildly irritating. He was most interested in economics and a serious critique of capitalism, which I found rather dry and abstract; my real interest was in culture, and day-to-day relationships between people. Even though I still knew little about Māori knowledge and culture, I believed that Māori were central to a new identity that was emerging in New Zealand. I was hazy about the details of the Treaty of Waitangi, even though I had spent time with my mates on protest marches, chanting 'The Treaty is a fraud!' The fact of Māori as tangata whenua made us different to the rest of the world, and with them lay possibilities for new thinking about ourselves. Māori offered something positive for our future – though I had no real idea what that might be.

A regular visitor in the Jesson family home was Donna Awatere. With the same intense demeanour I had observed in the Mt Eden prison visiting room, Donna sat talking with Bruce over the political papers that always crowded the Jessons' kitchen table. Bruce's familiarity with Black political writers, including the philosopher Frantz Fanon, helped enrich Donna's politics. It was a very unusual sight: a Māori woman and a Pākehā man, close together, engaging in serious intellectual discussion, sometimes for hours. Donna's singular focus made her frightening and attractive in equal measure. I still remember my timid and misguided question to Donna a couple of years earlier at the Piha Women's Liberation Congress. 'What can we Pākehā women do for Māori women?' She had skewered me with a look, and a swift reply: 'You Pākehā have to work it out for yourselves; we have enough to do with our own people.'

In the weeks and months that Donna sat engrossed in conversation with Bruce, she was writing the series of articles that would be published in the feminist magazine *Broadsheet*, and eventually form her book *Maori Sovereignty*, published in 1984. Her writing laid bare in the starkest terms her rage about the loss of 'the Maori right to determine our own destiny'.[11] The Treaty of Waitangi, she argued, was nothing to celebrate: it '[represented] the end of Maori sovereignty [and signalled] the swift rise to power of white people who would rule first by the gun, then by the police and prisons and then by their education, church and media'.[12] Addressing white feminists, she explained why Māori women were not enthusiastic about 'sisterhood'. Māori women's concerns, she declared, were not about the universal patriarchy, but about the fact 'that we and our people have no say in the shaping of our own destiny as a people. That rules in this country were made by immigrant races and nations, and were *not* made for the Maori and by the Maori.'[13]

Donna's unsettling articles were a direct challenge to us Pākehā feminists. In response, some of us who never liked the posturing moralism of identity politics formed a small group named Women for Aotearoa in 1982, to begin a series of meetings in the living rooms of our fashionably shabby Ponsonby houses. For me, the most significant thing was that, at last, we no longer needed overseas feminist or Marxist texts as the basis for our analysis. Māori sovereignty was a route to a critique of capitalism and poverty and power relations in New

Zealand. Māori writers emphasised groups over individuals, and environmental care rather than exploitation and money-making. We had found a politics that was uniquely New Zealand, *ours*.

Too busy to cook, we ate biscuits for our 'shared meals', and drank cups of tea as we earnestly debated how we Pākehā could support a Māori sovereignty movement. I was still happily inhabiting the realm of theoretical debate. I had no close Māori friends. Māori tended to have their own meetings. The few times Māori and Pākehā activist groups got together were fraught, with haranguing from Māori and defensiveness from Pākehā. I dreaded those meetings. I admired the Māori women I met in passing at protest events, but I had no idea how to talk to them. I felt intimidated; they were staunch, and unimpressed by Pākehā.

The most prominent radical Māori women were Donna Awatere, Ripeka Evans and Ngahuia Te Awekotuku. All had razor-sharp intellects and apparently boundless confidence. They knew the significance of appearance, too: they were photographed in dark clothing, with black boots, staunch shades and grim expressions, when most other activists cheerfully wore nondescript jeans and jerseys. The effect was as electrifying as they intended.

Mostly, I simply gazed at these women from a wary distance. I was glad of that distance; it was a safe spot from which to work out my ideas and to gain some of my own political confidence. My Pākehā friends and I knew that effective action required us to identify our *own* political interests, and not to act merely out of guilt about Māori criticisms.[14] I was not sure what our political interests were, but I did want to understand my own Pākehā-ness and New Zealand history. I was not ready, yet, to engage with Māori women politically as their equal, and in any case I could find no solid conduit for those relationships. Māori were working with Māori; we had to work it out for ourselves.

We joined Waitangi Day protests and Republican demonstrations against the 1983 royal visit, and planned a performance play to re-enact the Treaty on a local beach. The slogan 'the Treaty is a fraud' had morphed into 'honour the Treaty', as Māori recognised that the Treaty offered the only solid basis for negotiation. We made leaflets, wrote articles,[15] screen-printed dozens of little New Zealand flags with the Union Jack removed, and sewed a big cloth banner to carry in demonstrations.

I enjoyed being with my political friends, and I relished our spirited conversations. But I was not having a good time. We never laughed – everything was so earnest – and I suspected our meetings were just a talkfest and our actions largely pantomime. I wanted to have a self-deprecating belly laugh at us angst-ridden Pākehā, to guffaw at the stupidities and absurdities of human life.

When I saw Māori women together, I felt envious of their cheerfulness and apparent solidarity. They might have looked dangerous, but they knew how to laugh. Some Pākehā resented their humour, believing the laughter was directed at *us*, but I doubted they gave us much attention, and I did not mind even if they did find us ridiculous. The fact was that *I* found us ridiculous: we were so serious all the time, as we looked for the best political phrase and the most incisive analysis. I longed for such fun companions.

———

When I wasn't grinding my teeth in ghastly feminist meetings, I was self-righteous on a political moral high ground. With a new vocabulary that explained everything, I flung earnest criticisms far and wide, particularly at my hapless parents. My father, never a careful thinker, was an easy target. He said rape was about men wanting sex; I told him it was about male power. He said black people were not as smart as white people; I told him white people oppressed and dominated black people. He said poor people were poor because they were lazy; I told him the poor were necessary to a capitalist system that impoverished some in order to make others rich. He said Māori were lazy; I said that was racist. My excited ravings about the patriarchy, racism and capitalism only made my father say that I was 'ignorant' and, on one memorably hurtful occasion, 'a stupid cow'. He thought university had not done me any good; as he had predicted, it had just made me (more) argumentative and angry. Visiting my parents during the university holidays was not a happy experience.

No doubt I was insufferable. And I should have cut them some slack: their marriage was collapsing. My father's chronic depression and anxiety were suffocating him – and my mother, who was now looking for escape. In that generation, depression was seen as a personal failing, and my father's weakness further frayed my mother's already ragged patience. She had had enough of caring for Dad and raising five children, and now, responding to the mood of the era in which everyone was talking about women's liberation, she had decided to Do Something With Her Life. Her increasing independence made Dad even unhappier. He chewed his thumb raw. He spent his spare time in the Bethlehem garden, cutting down trees and planting new ones. Little wonder that know-it-all lectures from me were unwelcome.

———

Our serious political work went on. Our group decided to assist with the production of Donna Awatere's book *Maori Sovereignty*. We would provide the illustrations. It was an opportunity to 'work with Māori'. I was ambivalent because I found Donna's rhetoric far too sweeping. At the centre of her controversial articles was an explanation for the current social position of Māori – white hatred. She wrote: 'White hatred seems a harsh explanation for the attitudes of whites and for the way that the Maori has been and is being treated. But the evidence suggests that no other explanation will do.'[16]

I remember clearly my response to the idea of 'white hatred': it existed elsewhere, and had nothing to do with me. I had an image of rednecks, men who worked on farms and liked killing deer and rabbits, even though I knew nothing about what men like that actually thought about Māori. The phrase seemed showy, designed only to provoke. Donna later distanced herself from what she called this 'wrong, quite wrong' term, but at the time, it certainly got attention.[17] But it also stifled discussion; it was impossible to grasp, to give any nuance to. You could not argue against it – the evidence, Donna suggested, was necessarily everywhere. Everything could be explained in its terms: poor Māori education, health statistics, housing and poverty were all down to *race hatred*.

Like all unequivocal explanations, it allowed no room for discussion, complexity or analysis, so we just overlooked its over-the-top expression along with Donna's other extravagant flourishes about white evil, Satan and the Pākehā 'lizard's claws'. If she had said the conditions of Māori life were a product of *racism* rather than *hatred*, we might have nodded wisely, even though racism and white hatred are overlapping ideas. My view was that a more apt, and more hopeful, phrase might be white ignorance. Most Pākehā people seemed to know nothing about Māori history, and they did not even know that they did not know. In my experience, Pākehā like my father who denigrated Māori things knew nothing about Māori. On the other hand, I too knew next to nothing about Māori, though my ignorance was tempered by curiosity and attraction rather than rejection and fear.

I grew more impatient with the introduction of 'whiteness' into the conversation about Māori–Pākehā relationships in New Zealand. I had no doubt that racism was alive and kicking in New Zealand with regard to Māori, and terms such as 'white' were basic to conversations about racism, though of course we all struggled with 'Black' or 'brown' as the other term. To me, the term 'whites', and 'white racism' discussions, typically went nowhere with us Pākehā; they just curled back into anxiety and guilt. 'Whites' had become weaponised as describing unavoidably and downright *bad* people, and as such the term so often worked merely to close things down. I wanted us to talk about the idea of Pākehā – a relational term that opened up rather than suppressed possibilities. And anyway, I increasingly thought that the Māori struggle was not primarily an anti-racist one, whose solution was race equality. Donna, despite her language, seemed to address something more complex and nuanced: Māori authority and mana in their own country.

Because Donna's *Maori Sovereignty* text was largely angry rhetoric, it was not clear how we might illustrate it. We decided to write a sober parallel narrative using long captions beside historical photographs. At last I was forced to study New Zealand history. The six members of Women for Aotearoa spent hours sourcing photographs, and writing substantial captions telling the New Zealand story of British imperialism, forced land loss and Māori resistance, from the Treaty to the current time – underlying themes of Donna's book.

Researching those captions taught me much about the reasons for Māori anger. Like many New Zealanders who finally learn the facts of our country's colonisation, I felt outraged. It was impossible not to be appalled by the violence, lies and threats of the settler government and British forces in the 1860s; their invasion of the Waikato; their attack on the peaceful people of Parihaka in Taranaki; the assault on Maungapōhatu in Te Urewera – let alone the New Zealand government's confiscation of thousands of acres of tribal lands and distribution of them to Pākehā settlers; and its laws that broke up Māori collective land use, or that rated Māori land owners so heavily that they had to sell in order to pay what they owed to the state. I began to relate strongly to Donna's rage, thinking of my own parents when she wrote: 'They came here to this British farm in the Pacific, jobs waiting, preferential treatment, cultural recognition. And even then say, "Oh what happened to the Maori has got nothing to do with me". Christ Almighty!'[18] I love the exclamation mark and still grin in sardonic agreement at Donna's impatient indignation.

I think we enjoyed Donna's arguments mostly because they gave us much to be hopeful about:

> The Pakeha future in achieving a national identity can only be done with the Maori. It is the British way or the Maori way. These are your choices. The aim of Maori Sovereignty is not to achieve equality in white terms, but in Maori terms. ... The aim is to forge a distinctive New Zealand identity from a Maori point of view.[19]

Our collective future was 'with the Māori'. This sort of statement, which did not reject Pākehā, gave me hope that we could somehow work with Māori politically.

Donna wrote that 'the Maori people seek alliance with the white nation. In this way the interlocking racial unity of white people can be broken down and a new unity of Maori and Pakeha can be built up.'[20] One word stood out from her text: 'alliance' required no condemnation of others, and no goodies and baddies either. It seemed full of possibility, even if it was vague.

Alliances were all very well in theory, but Māori activists were not particularly interested. And they certainly did not welcome their alliances with Pākehā being made public. An assertion of Māori sovereignty was an assertion of independence, so in those touchy times no one mentioned the fact that Pākehā – Bruce Jesson and others, including Women for Aotearoa – had contributed significantly to this famous Māori sovereignty book.

Māori–Pākehā alliances, some of us joked ruefully at the time, were made by self-sacrificial Pākehā paddling hard at the rear of the waka, or making the sandwiches out the back, or writing reports over other people's names. 'What, you want *thanks*!?' said a Māori friend when she heard some moaning. 'Yes, sometimes!' I thought. But I never saw our unrecognised work as penance; it was in support of a wider cause. I knew that, to be successful, alliances with Māori had to be led by Māori. We were there in the relationship by invitation, and that came with some self-imposed limitations. We Pākehā rarely criticised Māori, for example, at least directly. I learned a valuable lesson when I stood up to a Māori woman, opposing good-naturedly some sweeping negative remark she had made; she took my response in good humour and I realised that positive argument with Māori activists was possible. Within this relationship, respecting someone could include disagreeing with them.

It is possible now to overlook the impact of *Maori Sovereignty*, to dismiss Donna's writing at that time as a simplistic diatribe. But her words, like those of other scholars and commentators such as Ranginui Walker, shifted Māori and Pākehā understandings of our colonial history. And Pākehā radical movements could no longer get away with simple abstractions like 'the workers', 'the people', 'women', 'families' or 'class society' in New Zealand without considering Māori.

———

Something else was changing. The language of race, which Black politics equated with colour, failed to take hold in New Zealand, not only for Pākehā like me, but also for Māori activists like Ripeka and Donna. They moved swiftly from identifying themselves as Black women to identifying as Māori, as tangata whenua, and, as a result, political relationships with Pacific cousins wilted. The Black category was being called on to do far too much, and could not contain the struggles of Pacific Islands people (already defined as Tongans, Samoans and so on) as well as the desire of some other 'non-whites', such as Indians, to come under the banner of Black struggles. And an explosion of Māori political activity, related to Māori land and Māori language, called Māori together to take up a strategically shared, historically rooted, political identity *as* Māori.

In all the conversations about race and white privilege I never considered myself 'a white', so the word felt like a term of analysis rather than identity. I understood the concepts of racism and white privilege, and how these applied to me as a white person, regardless of my personal politics. This privilege is manifest when you are ushered to the front of a post office queue in Tonga, when you notice that the kids in the New Zealand schools' top streams are almost all white, or when in the most expensive suburbs you rarely see a Polynesian. I recognised my membership of a privileged group and, it has to be said, I was (quietly) grateful for the benefits.

By now, all the discussion about Māori–Pākehā history had led me to a clear-eyed conclusion: I was a Pākehā. Even though Donna and other radical Māori used the term negatively ('the Pākehā stole the land'), I had come to embrace that term for myself, and I now claimed it proudly. Some acquaintances were scathing: 'Why are you using that word? It means "white flea". Or "bugger ya". Or "white potato" or something,' they sneered. 'And why use a Māori name for yourself, what's wrong with European New Zealander?' I had no idea what the Māori word 'Pākehā' meant, but I was not 'European' and I had never been to Europe. As a Pākehā, I felt lucky to have a place in the Māori world – even if only by name. I felt a solid sense of arrival in taking up that name and identity; that word anchored me in this part of the globe, in a permanent and necessary relationship with the indigenous people – even if I was not yet sure what that relationship might be.

———

All this time, I had been chipping away at my studies, gaining a postgraduate degree in the philosophy of education, and working as a university tutor to pay the rent. I was living in a flat in the inner-city suburb of Ponsonby, which was still being converted from a vibrant working-class area to a rather dull middle-class enclave – becoming, if I can use the language of colour, less brown and more white in the process. Our rented flat-fronted villa had polished kauri wood floors and wide-open sash windows, and we played Bob Dylan and Little Feat from our extensive vinyl collections.

In that house I met an intriguing visitor, William McCahon, the man I would marry and who would radically shape my aesthetic sense of being Pākehā.

Light on the kūmara garden

William was the eldest son of the artist Colin McCahon and his wife Anne. At the time I met him, I had not learned how to look at McCahon's paintings. I was yet to understand that his works were not to be viewed with a detached gaze; they demanded work – emotional, spiritual and intellectual. McCahon depicted a New Zealand of black and green, under sky that was by turns blinding white and forbidding black, and he used words, white words on a celestial blackboard. The mysteries of his paintings eluded me, though I was awed by their boldness and skewered by their beauty. But as my appreciation deepened under William's tutelage, McCahon began to transform the New Zealand landscape for me. I began to see, really see, the beautiful hills and the moody sea that I had previously regarded with admiration and familiarity. The place came alive with a strange newness, both brighter and darker than before, as if I had woken up from a long sleep.

McCahon's paintings would also teach me in my bones how to be a Pākehā, a person of *this* land. I was hungry for such teaching. I had been in my head, living on desiccated concepts and theories for so long that I fell upon the paintings and William's insights like a starving person. I relished our many walks and drives in the countryside, absorbing William's lessons in seeing.

I met his parents for the first time one evening at their

house in Grey Lynn, in 1977. Colin held court in the intimate
living room, interrogating – almost challenging – me with a
drunken directness. He was reading a book of Gerard Manley
Hopkins' poems and asked if I was familiar with the Victorian
poet's work. Luckily, I was. I could still remember being
enchanted as a schoolgirl by 'Glory be to God for dappled
things – / For skies of couple-colour as a brinded cow ...' but,
intimidated and star-struck, I had nothing much to say for
myself. William, his mother Anne and I listened as Colin read
poems aloud, repeating some of the phrases he found most
beautiful.

Two great works dominated the small room: a large chi–rho
monogram made of welded steel stood on the fireplace,[1] and,
above the sofa, a 1959 painting from McCahon's *Elias* series with
its divided landscapes of red, gold and blue under the scrawled
text 'will he come and save him will he save him. Elias will he
come to save him'. I sat between these two works, astonished
at their vitality; they both seemed to be speaking aloud, almost
drowning out Colin's reading. The *Elias* landscapes thundered
with their fierce questions: a grey gathering storm above a black
horizon, a dawn, roaring clouds, lucid pure blue water, troubled
red sky, and bright sunlight. Here, in this painting, I sensed
a lifetime of thinking and feeling. Later, I would comment
admiringly to Anne about the evocative desperation in the
shape of the words 'will he come and save him will he save him'.
Anne glanced up at the painting: 'Huh,' she said, in a tone more
resigned than bitter. 'He was drunk.'

William and I got into the habit of driving out to Muriwai
on the weekends to have lunch with Colin and Anne at their
bach, and then walking on the beach as William talked to me
about light and dark, about 'seeing through', making the solid

Learning to look at paintings at the Auckland Art Gallery, with husband
William McCahon. Our new son is strapped to my chest. *Alison Jones collection*

Above Our first son, Finn, was born in March 1981. He sat in a pram decorated with anti-tour slogans, as I marched against that winter's tour by the Springboks, the all-white South African rugby team. *Alison Jones collection*

Below William McCahon, Finn and I get involved in running a soup kitchen as a protest about poverty, during the Royal Tour of 1983. *Alison Jones collection*

With William McCahon and our son Finn, in Auckland in 1982. *Photograph by Lesley Phillips, Alison Jones collection*

My mother's 'lost' family about 1914 in England. My grandmother, Janet Story, aged seventeen, is on the far right. Later, Janet would secretly place her illegitimate new-born daughter in an orphanage. That child, my mother, was not told about her origins, something that always troubled her. We eventually found Janet, but she refused to recognise Ruth as her daughter. Ruth later met her half-sister, Monica, in New Zealand, and connection was made between the families. When I saw this photograph, I was shocked at my resemblance to my grandmother as a young woman. *Alison Jones collection*

Above Teaching my first feminist theory class around 1986. The students and I were constructing a chart of theoretical ideas on a piece of butcher's wrapping paper attached to the wall. I later taught this class with Kuni Kaa Jenkins and it expanded to include mana wāhine. *Alison Jones collection*

Below Kuni Kaa Jenkins, one of the students, contributes to the discussion in the feminist theory class. In these classes I learned with, and from, my students. *Alison Jones collection*

Above Teaching around 1986. Egalitarian teaching was the style, with the teacher often sitting alongside the students. Linda Tuhiwai Smith is the student speaking; I am on the right. *Alison Jones collection*

Below Teaching feminist theory at the University of Auckland around 1986. *Alison Jones collection*

Above Our university classes were intense and engaged, and I usually held our final class at one of the students' homes where we continued to debate our ideas. *Alison Jones collection*

Below Kuni and I spent time in the Bay of Islands to research the early Māori establishment of schooling. This led us to the story of Tuai, a young Ngare Raumati leader who travelled to England and worked on the first Māori grammar. This view of the bay, looking north from Tāpeka near Tuai's kāinga, was painted by the British artist Augustus Earle. Entrance to the Bay of Islands, New Zealand, *watercolour by Augustus Earle, 1827, National Library of Australia, nla.obj-134503539*

Kuni Kaa Jenkins and I share a joke in 2018. We both feel awkward as we pose for the photograph inside the meeting house on the University of Auckland's Waipapa marae. When we taught together in the 1990s, we often used this wharenui as a teaching space. *Photograph by Simon Young, taken for Margie Thomson and Simon Young,* Womankind: New Zealand Women Making a Difference, *Penguin Books, Auckland, 2019*

translucent and the translucent solid. For the first time, I saw the black in the New Zealand landscape – not only in the hills and shadows, but also at the edges of the land and the sea. McCahon's canvas panels series named *Walk* transformed every afternoon stroll on Muriwai Beach – in rain, storm or sun – into a spiritual experience, transcendent, delightful. In *Walk*, McCahon's layered lines of the horizon, of bird footsteps, of the clouds and the waves spoke, one to the other, and to me, about their divine place in the universe.

William's conversations drew on some of the knowledge gained from his father. Throughout his childhood, he and his siblings had accompanied their parents on journeys of seeing. Colin drove the family car, stopping on roadsides where everyone would be obliged to sit, observing the landscape – its light and dark, its horizontals and verticals, its stasis and fluidity, and its moods and spirits. As well as rendering this landscape in startlingly original ways, McCahon sometimes placed in that landscape symbols from the Christian Church, bringing the familiar ancient images to confront us here at home. For some New Zealanders, this was heresy; for others a revelation.

I never felt that McCahon's crucifixions in Canterbury or angels in the New Zealand hills had much to do with the conventions of mainstream Christianity. For me, the paintings provoked a sense of mysterious and unseen energies, which could be expressed with any number of different iconographies. It was clear in some of McCahon's paintings that he not only sought to speak of spiritual forces through Christian imagery, but that he sensed Māori atua in the land.

One painting that referred to atua was *May His light shine (Cornwall Park)*, which depicted the mountain, One Tree Hill.

In this arresting canvas, across the black face of the rounded hill were the words 'HE'S The ONE may his Light shine on the Kumara Garden'. Inscribed in small writing below: 'Kumara god set in concrete, Cornwall Park', and a phrase derived from a Gerard Manley Hopkins poem, 'Mine Thou Lord of Life send my roots rain'.[2]

Perhaps because I had been born in the shadow of this black mountain, when I first saw the work in a 1980 exhibition I was held by its presence. It returned me to my romantic thoughts about Maungakiekie, and the doubled sense of the land, Māori and Pākehā. McCahon seemed to have captured my thinking and laid it on canvas, confronting me with more questions and suggesting the possibilities in a deeper relationship with my (literal) birthplace. I puzzled over the words and symbols in the painting. Was the kūmara god, the god of the ancient Waiohua kūmara gardens, the block of wood, standing at the base of the hill? Or is the god in the white post at the summit splitting the orange evening sky, letting in the white light of another world beyond this one? A subtle political message seemed to be at work in the painting as well. Both posts – whether of European block manufacture, metal or concrete – suggest interference in Māori life that may need a celestial remedy from *Thou Lord of Life* or the light of *The One*.

Never had my brain and feelings worked so hard together as they did in the excited struggle with this work: it demanded attention, it eschewed conclusion, it was generous in its presence. I was not distracted by the idea of Him or the Lord. The religious language was simply a placeholder for something *other*, the realm of the spiritual.

I was by now gaining an appreciation of a spiritual realm through being at Māori events. It was becoming obvious to me that I could not begin to understand the Māori world if I was not open to the idea of spiritual forces. I was judgmental about Māori prayers to a Christian God, apt to dismiss them as simply colonised thinking. But being critical was not useful; being interested in the Māori world did not require me to critique it.

Māori say karakia, whether addressing a Christian God or the atua, at almost any opportunity – and especially, in my experience, before eating, and at the beginning and end of meetings. As a confirmed atheist, I would make shopping lists in my head to pass the time during long prayers. But then I began to wonder about karakia. I felt, rather than understood, their significance. They were, I realised, not about an individual communion with God but were part of a collective social experience. Prayers at the beginnings of meetings served to slow down time, to draw together the people in the room, to bring a collective focus on what they were doing. The karakia called in all the forces of emotion, attention and knowledge needed to make the meeting a success. Regardless of the words and what they meant, the karakia became for me a few minutes to contemplate something I rarely recognised: the entanglements of elements of social life with the *something else* – the world outside us humans. The only non-Māori situation where I could get a sense of that *something else* was in McCahon's paintings.

When William and I discussed *May His light shine*, William suggested that the kūmara god shaped as a post was a 'god stick' representing Rongo, the god of cultivation. Colin used to visit the so-called god sticks at the Auckland Museum, and William took me on a special trip to look at them. We found the 'sticks' stacked in a dingy corner behind glass. These six long plain staffs, toko, had eluded my attention on other museum visits because I was far more taken by the highly decorated waka and the wild-eyed carvings filling the Māori section. The toko are smooth lengths of wood, each knobbed at the top, and carved into subtle, and achingly beautiful, abstract shapes, each embodying great elements or atua.[3] William told me that toko were used for teaching about the fundamental forces of the world, such as the tides and the winds, as well as human activity such as cultivation. The museum's toko had been found buried near Auckland by a Pākehā farmer who had cut the long staffs into shorter lengths for storage.

Standing before these taonga, mesmerised by their simple shapes, I felt tears come to my eyes. I felt for the imprisoned toko, for the human skill that had shaped their delicate curves, for the intellectual ideas that formed them, and the haunting chants that would have accompanied their formation and use. Their brutal truncation and their relegation to a museum corner seemed utterly sad.

Yet despite their desolate location, the toko seemed to hold their power defiantly, permanently and with utter certainty. I could not help but feel their spiritual presence. Their simple shapes seemed to possess the whole world: all its strengths, beauty and hurts, all its human genius and stupidity.

My life with William and the McCahon family was a period of such intensity that its eventual demise was perhaps not surprising. William and I would eventually separate in 1993. But the sixteen years of our marriage helped make possible a spiritual sensibility essential for my developing engagement with Māori.

———

Our first son, Finn, was born in March 1981. He sat in a pram
decorated with anti-tour slogans, as I marched against that
winter's tour by the Springboks, the all-white South African
rugby team. With the rest of a group called 'Jellyfish Against
the Tour' made up of old people, the disabled, nuns, children
and mothers, I took to the streets on designated routes well
away from the dangerous police lines. William and his friends,
joining the squads nearer the front, had to wear their motorbike
helmets and cardboard body armour to avoid injury from police
batons. It was a frightening time.

The intensity of the anti-tour protests – and the violence
of the police response – shocked everyone and split the
already-fractured Jones family as it brought to a head the
long-simmering tension between me and my father and
brothers about sporting contacts with a country ruled by
an apartheid regime. My two brothers supported the rugby,
believing that 'politics should be kept out of sport'. Our father
agreed, dismissing my opinions as ignorant. We argued bitterly.
One brother tried to say that because I had never been to South
Africa I had no right to have an opinion about that country's
apartheid politics. I retorted that most of us had never been to
Hitler's Germany, either, which did not stop us all condemning
that regime.

On the day of the final game, the third test in Auckland
on 12 September, I was pushing my son's pram up and down
the streets of Ponsonby, pacing quickly to calm the feeling of
dread that something horrible would happen to William and
our friends who had kitted themselves up for the day's protest,
which was to be the tour's most violent. Fighting erupted in
streets near the rugby venue, and police pelted with rocks and
missiles gave as good as they got. The protesters seemed to

have been joined by opportunists keen to fight the police. I saw a small plane above the Mt Eden ground, buzzing and dipping and circling, and felt my worries intensify. I would later learn the hired plane was piloted by a man we knew, Marx Jones, who with a friend dropped flour bombs on the rugby field. The plane was a prophetic cross in the sky, like McCahon's crucifix-plane flying over Muriwai Beach. Although I had never experienced war where death comes from the sky, I felt the hollow shock of social dislocation. It seemed that, here in New Zealand, we were at war.

It was a war on sacred ground – it is no exaggeration to say that rugby was akin to a religion in New Zealand – pitting rugby supporters against those who wanted to denounce the racism of apartheid. Although many Māori were in support of the rugby, Māori leaders well known in both Māori and Pākehā communities spoke out against the tour, sometimes shocking their respectable Pākehā friends who believed we should support rugby come-what-may. I found out later that my school friend Rāhera's father, a Māori leader widely admired in Tauranga, had lost a number of prominent Pākehā friends over his opposition to the rugby ties with South Africa.

––––––

Although I adored my child, I was bored by the routines of motherhood. I felt a need to continue studying, and I successfully applied for a doctoral scholarship at the university, just enough to support our small family. But what to study? One of my feminist friends had a daughter with African heritage who was experiencing difficulties at secondary school. She insisted that I study 'racism in schools'. As usual, I baulked at the term racism; it seemed such a blunt tool to pry open a problem.

Instead, I began to read what I could find about how schools benefit some kids and not others.

Marxist theory was fashionable then, and inspiring for its insights into how schools work to maintain the existing social and economic hierarchies. Most educational research seemed focused on how to make schools work *better*, but Marxist writers asked what schools were working *for*. Who, they enquired, gained most from schooling and how? I got permission from the progressive principal of nearby Auckland Girls' Grammar School, Charmaine Pountney, to do some research in the classroom. I wanted to track exactly how the working-class Pacific Islands girls ended up getting relatively poor marks and low-paying jobs, even if they worked hard at school and followed the teachers' instructions.

And so I went back to school. But this time, instead of being in the top stream amongst Pākehā peers, I was in the lowest stream, with the Pacific Islands (and a few Māori) girls. They were mystified at my interest in them; I tried to explain what research was. I followed them around the playground, even when they played truant, smoking in the toilets of a nearby park during school hours. Of course, they barely tolerated me and often ran away or hid when I sought them out. It was hard work keeping up with them, particularly when I was not even sure what I was looking for.

After months at the back of classrooms, carefully watching how the girls approached their schoolwork, I realised something that surprised me. These girls and their teachers seemed to work unconsciously together to ensure the girls' poor performance. The girls displayed an insistent and uncritical respect for authority and demanded to be taught directly ('Give us the notes, Miss'; 'What is the answer, Miss?'). The teachers tended to 'give the notes' to placate their students, and keep them happily doing what the girls thought was schoolwork. I began to realise that this was (partly) how the school failed them: the school rewarded critical and independent thought, not memory and conformity. In bowing to these Pacific girls' conformist cultural demands and their respectful notion of being taught (that is, by giving them some power over classroom teaching, aka culturally responsive pedagogy), the school might have been teaching the hard-working Pacific girls, but it was never going to reward them.[4]

This seemed alarmingly complicated. I was rapidly becoming even more suspicious of simple analyses, such as 'Teachers oppress Pacific students! Schools are racist places!' I developed a tolerance for complexity even though it meant I was not toeing a clear party line. I was surrounded by people who chanted simple political slogans, with supposedly simple political solutions – Equality! Anti-racism! Down with capitalism! I agreed with their sentiments in broad terms, but they were failing to even begin to grapple with the complexities of the power dynamics under-pinning and maintaining social advantage and disadvantage.

———

When Finn turned four in early 1985, we decided that he should learn the Māori language. I remembered the palangi children in Tonga who, playing with the local kids, learned the language quickly. I regretted not having had the childhood opportunity to learn te reo myself, and was keen for Finn to have the chance. My hope was that he would be part of a new generation of Pākehā kids who would have decent relationships with Māori and would help revive a language under serious threat.

Near our house was a new Māori-language preschool, a
kōhanga reo. Māori communities had been alarmed by a survey
on the woeful state of the language,[5] and dozens of kōhanga
reo (language nests) for preschool children were now opening
across the country. The first had opened only three years
before, in Wainuiomata in 1982, and by now there were 400
across the country.[6] Our local Richmond Road School, still a
reflection of older Ponsonby before the inflow of Pākehā, had
a majority of Māori and Pacific Islands children. It was a centre
of progressive education and the Māori principal and his
supporters – after a considerable political struggle – had gained
official permission to establish a kōhanga reo.[7]

Two unused prefabricated buildings were to be converted
into kōhanga classrooms, and parents with carpentry skills
volunteered to work in the weekends. William got involved, and
found some beautiful slabs of kauri from which to make little
stools for the children's toilets.

The school community who worked on the building turned
out to be a group of local Pākehā parents who had the kind
of political verve that made me both laugh with incredulity
and cry with frustration. I think they must have read up on
Māori traditional cultural norms and found that women were
apparently not allowed on building sites. So we women were
banned from the sawing and hammering, and relegated to the
school kitchen to make and serve the food.

This could hardly have offended my feminist principles
more deeply, but I capitulated, uncertain about criticising
'traditional culture'. I did not know enough to even begin to
assess whether this was in fact a traditional rule, and whether
a non-carved re-purposed classroom prefab was exempt. And
why should we, all Pākehā radicals, worry about tradition? Most

significantly, I did not have Māori women friends with whom I
could discuss my misgivings. By now, I had only two good Māori
mates, both men who were William's friends, Buster the artist
(Tom Pihama aka Buster Black, whose black, textured paintings
had inspired his teacher Colin McCahon), and good-hearted
Bunny, both of whom avoided politics and controversy. We saw
each of them regularly, and I tried to discuss my annoyance.
Bunny laughed with glee, without offering an opinion, and
Buster just said 'Bullshit! Do what you want,' and showed no
further interest.

Not only were women barred from the kōhanga building
site, but it was decided that we (all atheists) must have a Māori
prayer, a karakia, recited before eating. No one knew how to say
a karakia, so every Saturday at lunchtime, one of the women
in the kitchen would call in a local Māori child playing in the
playground. The child was required to summon the men from
their work, and then to come and chant a karakia for us.

In hindsight, the whole scene was quite funny, and maybe
even sweet: a group of earnest Pākehā parents building a
Māori-language school, with a random Māori child guiding us
on protocol. Nevertheless, I was irritated at our pedantic – or
at least undiscussed – following of arcane rules about women's
work and about prayers.

———

When the kōhanga classrooms were completed, we enrolled
Finn. There were repercussions. I was visited at home by two
Pākehā women, members of the (non-) building team. They said
they were 'committed to challenging Pākehā racism', under the
guidance of a Māori group to whom they reported their good

deeds. One of the women had changed her name from Hannah
to the more Māori-sounding Hana.

Hana and her friend had come to 'talk about the kōhanga'. I
offered the visitors tea and homemade carrot cake at our house,
which looked like every other young Pākehā couple's house
in Ponsonby then: unpainted plasterboard, walls knocked
out to make bigger spaces around a pot-belly stove, books on
makeshift brick-and-board shelves, comfy sofas and children's
paintings on display. We drank the tea and ate the cake, and
made small talk about my doctoral research.

Hana then got to the point: 'Why are you sending your
Pākehā child to the kōhanga reo?' 'Why not?' I replied, 'I want
him to speak Māori!' 'You are taking a place from a Māori child
who could be learning their own language, and you should
withdraw him.' I had not heard there was a waiting list; Hana
confirmed there was not one. 'If there is no waiting list, then
what is the problem?' Hana persisted – the revitalisation of
Māori language was not for Pākehā, all resources had to go
towards getting Māori children to the kōhanga. It is quite
simple, she concluded, triumphantly.

I countered that all of us should speak Māori. Pākehā
support for the language is a crucial part of its revitalisation,
I said, and the more Māori-speaking kids, the merrier! 'And I
would rather talk to Māori about it, thanks,' I added, pointedly.
Hana had a ready reply: 'Well, it is up to Pākehā to challenge
Pākehā. Māori should not have to do it; they have enough to do
already.' I was ruefully reminded of the feminist arguments I had
used myself: don't talk to men about feminism, put your energy
into women. Why should Māori educate Pākehā when they had
plenty of Māori to be talking to?

As politely as I could I told her to bugger off. I felt both rage that I was being policed, and humiliation that I had been caught without a thought-through position. Again, I regretted that I did not have Māori women friends with whom to discuss these things. I had lost touch with Ripeka. The only Māori women I encountered, even fleetingly, were Donna Awatere, the Ngāti Whātua activist Sharon Hawke, and Merata Mita the film-maker: staunch, distant, forbidding women, with more important matters to attend to.

I raised the question of Pākehā learning te reo Māori at a feminist political meeting a few weeks later, after a rant by Rena, a newly politicised Māori woman who – annoyingly – assumed that we Pākehā had not heard of social class, racism or feminism before. Rena was in no mood for discussion; she simply asserted that Pākehā should *not* be part of Māori language revitalisation. I dropped the whole thing, although I did feel troubled about the implications of some Pākehā becoming more fluent in te reo Māori than some Māori, and whether this was another form of colonisation. In the meantime, Finn had been welcomed at the kōhanga into a class of fifteen Māori children, and two Pākehā.

At Richmond Road kōhanga the children sat in rows, cross-legged, on the floor for long periods of time, chanting and repeating words and songs. The teacher, like most of the other kaiako of kōhanga in the country, was an unpaid Māori-speaking kuia. Mirroring her own schooling experiences, she carried a pointing stick. We parents were clear that while old-fashioned teaching was okay, old-fashioned school discipline was not.

Finn assumed that sitting and repetition was what 'school' was all about, and he did learn to speak some Māori and picked up some action songs – his skinny white torso made a hilariously stark contrast with the robust brown bodies of his classmates as they performed their end-of-year haka and waiata. Life was ticking along just fine. I was busy writing my doctorate, and Finn seemed cheerful.

———

Things changed when, at five, Finn graduated to the bilingual section of the school. He had been protected in the kōhanga reo because the preschool children did not join the older pupils in the playground. Despite his skilled and affectionate new Māori teacher, he now refused to go to school. Each morning he cried and raged, and I peeled him out of the car, forcing him in to the school grounds. On really bad days, William and I allowed him to stay home from school. He would not reveal the problem.

One afternoon I noticed red welts on his legs. He reluctantly told me that some boys in the playground whipped him with paspalum stalks, calling him 'honky'. He whimpered: 'I am not a honky, am I Mum?' I had to break the news to him: yes, indeed, he was a honky, a white person. He thought he was a Māori because he spoke Māori. He cried, disappointed that he was not a Māori after all. It broke my heart to see him so unhappy.

The next day I went to see the new principal. The beloved previous principal had died, and the man I met was hostile from the moment I walked into his office. He knew he was facing a bolshie, articulate Pākehā mother. I reported that Finn was being bullied because he was a Pākehā, and the reply was sharp: 'I can't worry about your child. He is from a middle-class family and he will be fine.' Angry and indignant, I told him that he had no grasp on the future of 'us all getting on together', and that bullying was never acceptable, regardless of its logic. I transferred Finn to another local school that, sadly, had fewer Māori children.

The barriers that had been erected to Finn's access to Māori language and Māori classmates made me seethe, but I tried not to personalise them. My idealistic desires were for all children, and adults, to learn the indigenous – and official – language of the country, but the practicalities were complicated. Radical ideologies had taken root that operated on the assumption of a zero-sum game: Māori could only get more if Pākehā got less. After all, it had been the other way around for two centuries. It was impossible to disagree with *that;* any thinking person knew that Māori had been systematically robbed of their land and lost their language while Pākehā systematically benefited, and that Pākehā – sometimes with good intentions, though more often with greed and a desire for domination – were to blame. But however much I understood and accepted Māori anger, I could not accept that individual hostility was useful in the long term.

Wānanga

I had been making sporadic attempts to learn Māori for years, going to night classes, learning basics, forgetting, and starting again. I never seemed to get beyond the beginners' level. Now that I had completed my PhD and was working as a lecturer at the University of Auckland, I felt embarrassed at work when colleagues spoke to me in te reo and I replied in English. Understanding the language was one thing; speaking it was quite another. If someone in the staff kitchen asked casually 'He pai ō rā whakatā?' (Did you have a good weekend?) I would baulk at wasting their time as I stuttered through a reply, 'Ae, he tino pai ōku rā whakatā!' (Yes, my weekend was very good!). I could fluently recite a ritual greeting 'Tēnā koutou katoa. Ka nui te mihi ki a koutou kua tae mai nei i tēnei ata' (hello to you who have come here this morning), but I could not cope confidently with a simple conversation.

I decided to enrol in an immersion course at Te Wānanga o Aotearoa, in South Auckland. My friends were impressed, commending me for my 'bravery'. I have often noticed an unpleasant competitiveness among Pākehā about competence in the Māori world, and my going to the wānanga was regarded with some envy. Many saw me as heading into a sphere they wanted access to, but felt too daunted or anxious or busy to enter.

Some added that they were troubled by what they saw as the sexism of formal Māori protocols that required that men

sit in the front row on the marae and forbade women to make
formal speeches on the paepae. I can't say that rule bothered
me, not least because it removed any pressure on me to speak.
In any case, the women were always quick to share their views
under their breath about the male speakers, which created
an enjoyable solidarity in the back row. I knew the women
were powerful behind the scenes. I also accepted that Māori
protocols were based in valued Māori cultural tradition, even
if that tradition had sometimes been affected by European
patriarchal ideals. If change was sought, it was up to Māori
women, and not an outsider.

To make room for the four-day-a-week classes, I reduced
my work hours at the university. But I felt more nervous than
excited. I secretly knew that what I was doing was both too
little and too late. I was too old to master a new language. And
I expected to be near the bottom of this class. I bought a CD
of waiata to play in the car. For a year, four mornings a week, I
battled through the morning traffic from my inner-city home to
Māngere, through the poor and unfamiliar suburbs of Manukau,
down suburban streets with their few trees and dried-up lawns.
Past Pak'nSave, KFC and Burger King, to the modern buildings
of the wānanga.

On the first day, there was a huge pōwhiri in the car park for all
the students – returning and new – and their families. Standing at
the back of the crowd of hundreds, I could not hear the speakers
or see the front. There were few Pākehā, and I saw no one I knew.
We later met our teachers and the library and support staff: 'May
God bless you all as we journey together in this education world,'
said one, enthusiastically. Amen to that, I thought.

I found the room number on a noticeboard, then wandered
around, struggling with my tendency towards anxiety-induced

myopia. By the time I finally found where I was meant to be, others were already inside, talking in English and laughing. Gravitating towards the familiar, I sat down next to an older woman. She introduced herself as Mere ('My name was Violet but I'm not a Violet') and I liked her immediately. She was in her late seventies, and a whaea in her community up north. She said she felt anxious, too, and that she was desperate to learn Māori. 'All the old people are dead now. It is up to us and we know nothing. The younger ones know more than us!' Her story was familiar: her schoolteachers had refused to allow her to speak Māori and her parents, both fluent speakers, actively discouraged her because they believed it would impede her success in a world dominated by English. 'They thought that was the best for us, and now we can't do what they did on the marae,' she said with poignant resignation.

There were nineteen of us in the class, seventeen Māori and two Pākehā, ranging in age from eighteen to seventy-four. Most came from South Auckland. One man let us know he was 'in the business world', and that 'Māori, including all my relations, have to front up, stop taking welfare, and get off their arses'. No one appeared bothered by this viewpoint, though I bristled quietly. Emma said she had changed her surname to Clark because Pākehā couldn't pronounce Karaka. An older woman had three mokopuna to care for, including two with foetal alcohol syndrome. One, who looked after her terminally ill father, had a serious heart condition herself. Someone's small rented two-bedroom house contained three large families. The other Pākehā was a schoolteacher looking for a new flatmate; the last one stole her stuff.

No one was self-pitying. Except me. My own situation – one couple in a three-bedroom house – seemed almost wickedly selfish. But I was simply being the tragedy queen of my own universe – self-absorbed, inward-looking. This tendency to feel guilty about my privilege had little value, I soon discovered. I learned to identify, then laugh at and dismiss, my own self-focused anxieties, while never forgetting my own social power and the benefits I gained from it daily.

Some of my classmates were curious about why a Pākehā would want to learn Māori. Although I declared to Mere, and to Rāwiri and Rachael, that every New Zealander should have a command of at least everyday te reo, they were not convinced. Rāwiri made the not-unreasonable point that the language 'is so impractical for a Pākehā – when would you use it?'. Rachael said with a smile that she suspected I was 'a closet Māori', though I wasn't sure what that might be. Mere sought my assistance as she grappled with unfamiliar classroom tasks; once she whispered in English, the forbidden language: 'I want to learn Māori from just sitting here.' I had tried the osmosis approach myself. At home, I listened to Māori Television hoping vainly that the language would magically take up residence in my brain.

I was alarmed by the teacher's basic rules, the rules of the Ataarangi Method of teaching Māori: kaua e kōrero Pākehā (don't speak English), and whakarongo, titiro, kōrero, that is, learn through listening, observing and speaking. We were not to use books or take notes or look for words in our dictionaries. Having spent my whole educational life completely dependent on the written word, I was desperate to take notes, to find and record unfamiliar words, so I propped up a dictionary and a notepad out of sight under my desk. I sat far away from the teacher. I avoided her gaze, and remained silent. I behaved like a scared kid in school.

Time in these classes took on a different dimension. Everything seemed to happen in slow motion and the students were often in charge, though no one else seemed to mind. I had to just relax and let it all unfold. The teacher did not intervene; she sat impassively, arms folded. I could not tell if she was annoyed, amused or just plain tired. I noticed that men like Toka seemed fluent Māori speakers in a formal context like a pōwhiri or a karakia, but when it came to learning the language rules bit by bit, or saying 'the sheep were chased by the dog' and 'who has my pencil?', they found it impossible. And when a younger woman prompted him in a language game, Toka got openly hostile. I felt for him, but was fearful of his anger too.

I could tell from their private jokes that some of the younger women found their elders' behaviour exasperating and funny, but in class they were straight-faced and respectful. And I had to stop myself from crossly growling at seventy-four-year-old Ronnie when, having grasped the wrong end of the stick in our small group sessions, he insisted on telling us what to do.

As the weeks went by, I painstakingly and painfully learned verbs, tenses, grammar rules and vocabulary – and promptly forgot them. My mistakes and ignorance and poor memory made me burn with humiliation. When I tried to scribble down notes, the eagle-eyed teacher reminded me, 'Whakatakoto te rākau!' (Put down your pencil!). When she singled me out with a question or comment in te reo, my words felt like marbles in my mouth.

At night, I had nightmares about being lost and confused. In one dream, my neighbour's house had been purchased by a senior person from the wānanga, who had built mansion-like extensions that kept coming further towards my small house until they extended right inside it and I did not know where my house began and ended. Returning home, I would be perplexed about how to get into the house. I always did have rather obvious dreams.

———

Despite my private anxieties, I kept going to class. Mere relied on me and I was being inexorably drawn into the group. If I missed a day, my classmates would interrogate me on my return. They were not so much being nosy as assuming that my business was their business, that each of us was responsible for the others, as well as being responsible to the others. Even so, people would be absent from our small group activities when we all relied on each other. Those absent without a good excuse would become the focus of merciless jokes. It was a complicated dance in which we all participated; there was no way to stand on the sidelines because everyone was relentlessly included. An individual arriving late to class had to sing as a punishment. Everyone would join in with gusto, so there was no discomfort for the latecomer. The slowest people in the class were uniformly encouraged, even if they never managed to get anything correct. This atmosphere of relaxed positivity benefited everyone and I was struck by the paradox that Māori collectivism foregrounds the individual in that each individual is actively included. Pākehā individualism, on the other hand, effaces the individual, who must keep up or be left behind.

Even though I felt part of the group, I was, inevitably, on the outside of the others' social world. The conversations in illicit English among the women before and after class were about things beyond my sphere: local kōhanga reo politics, tangihanga of people I did not know, hapū and community gossip, basketball, touch rugby, kapa haka, drinking parties, hospital emergencies, television programmes, new tattoos, people in prison.

For Rachael, I was a conduit to new knowledge. She asked me to teach her about 'new Pākehā words', like 'implicit' and 'synonym'. She had never heard of the extinct huia bird, and asked me why people talked about the Treaty of Waitangi and what I thought of the Prime Minister. She laughed at my need to write everything down in class, and was mystified by my reliance on a dictionary. She had a great memory, and learned a lot faster than I did.

I was learning about being 'in the everyday' amongst Māori. I greeted acquaintances each morning with a casual kiss, or a hongi. It was quite common for someone to come in late and still take the time to warmly greet every classmate. All decisions were made with others. No one ever announced they were going out that weekend by themselves; no one ever seemed to do *anything* for or by themselves. When Manuka turned up to class with lollies in $2 packets to raise money for his mokopuna's kōhanga reo, I donated $10, with no intention of actually taking the lollies. When he offered me the five packets I said 'Ngā mihi. He koha. Kāore au e hiahia. I don't want them. You resell them.' Rachael and Ana-Lisa, sitting next to me, did not hesitate: 'We'll have them,' and passed the sweets around the room. Considering only yourself was not thinkable in this group. I knew that if my elderly mother were to die, for instance, the group would take a day to come to her funeral, even though they had never met her.

Strong emotion was never far beneath the surface in the

class. We rarely got through a day without some intense feeling: a spontaneous song (sad or happy), loud laughter, silent tears, quickly rising hostility, sullen glances, silences, pūkana, smart comments, jokes, gossip, arguments. Nothing was straightforward. And yet, by the end of each day, we returned to an even keel and after the final karakia left (usually) with good feelings all round. The group felt like a family, with all its complexities. However irritating someone might be, we all stuck together.

Singing and laughter made the glue that connected us. Everyone loved to sing, at any time or place. Toka always had his guitar on hand. Most of all, I loved the constant enthusiasm for wordplay, and all the jokey made-up words that pepper Māori language in common use: hāwhe pai (half pie); miki api (mixed up), maka raoni (muck around); inawhi rumi (enough room); palani pī (Plan B); katie pie (kei te pai). My favourite was tītautanga (tea towel tanga – rules of the kitchen).

The Māori language has absorbed countless words from English just by simple and sometimes playful mimicking, like kau for cow, miraka for milk, pae kare (by golly) and harirū, a transliteration of 'how do you do?' for a handshake. Despite some scholarly disapproval, people just go ahead with transliterations and the everyday language changes. Tūreiti (a transliteration of 'too late') is a common and funny way of describing a latecomer, allowing tardy students to laughingly introduce themselves as Ngāti Tūreiti (from the tribe Tūreiti). But not all new words are transliterations. Creative new vocabularies have emerged – a process that started from the first contact with the European world – to name modern technologies: computers are rorohiko, literally brain (roro) lightning flash (hiko); digital is matihiko, with mati meaning finger; waea pūkoro is cellphone, from a transliteration of 'wire' and pūkoro, pocket.

With a sudden shock of realisation, I recalled the words we used commonly as children without knowing they were Māori: cock-a-bully (kōkopu, small freshwater fish); e-haw (e hoa, friend); pucka-roo (pākaru, broken); boo-eye (Pūhoi, referring to a distant place); biddy-bid (piripiri, a sticky seed); Jack-naw-hee (nohi, a Māori pronunciation of nosy); worry or warry (whare, a hut, small house).

Every day, a new aspect of the language came into view. The onomatopoeia was always fun: kihikihi, cicada; katakata, laugh; ketekete, click the tongue; kōmuhumuhu, murmur. Repetition of sounds often intensified them: kare is a ripple, karekare describes a choppy sea; kata is laugh, and katakata is to giggle and laugh a lot; kōrero is talk and kōrerorero, conversation. I noticed that single words had many subtleties of meaning, only properly understood in context. The Pākehā tendency to find a single meaning for a word just does not work. For example, the lovely soft word pae can refer to horizon, perch, step, orator's bench, shelf, circumference, or mountain range. Aroha is commonly taken to mean 'love'. Yet the word refers to a variety of feelings towards others, including sympathy, apology, pity, compassion, empathy and respect – depending on who is speaking and why.

My language discoveries did not impress one Pākehā friend who insisted the language was limited if it could not 'say what it meant' – that is, if word meanings were multiple and flexible rather than fixed and reliable. I could not agree; for me, the subtlety of meaning-in-context was intriguing. It forced me to understand that, for Māori, language binds speaker and listener (and the environment) together as they create shared meaning in the moment of their communication. And multiple meanings easily lend themselves to metaphor and to the skilful and humorous language-play so often present in Māori contexts.

———

In my year of the wānanga, I merely skimmed the language's surfaces. Yet even in the simplest lessons I found new insights. I noticed how sentence structures assumed and expressed a different way of thinking – that is, how language carries culture.

The Māori language has no equivalent of 'to be' or 'to have' in its simple sense. I learned that the simple sentence 'I have no trousers' was 'kāore ōku tarau' (none my trousers), and was immediately intrigued. My trousers are in a state of not-being-had. And in English, we use a verb to connect a noun and its adjective: 'This apple is sour.' But in te reo, 'is' or 'are' or 'was' do not intervene: 'he kawa tēnei āporo' (sour this apple). The apple and its sourness are one. Plus, the sourness, kawa, comes first in the sentence, as though the state is more salient than the thing. The apple directly possesses its quality of sourness. I am interested in this apparent difference: between our English-language tendency to classify the object, and the Māori-language tendency towards a sense of an object's agency (in these examples, the apple's own sourness and the trousers' own not-there-ness). In English we say 'she is beautiful.' In Māori, 'he ātaahua ia' (beautiful she). The beauty and she are indivisible. The actor – she, ia – appears last in any such sentence, with the effect of foregrounding the state of things, rather than their naming.

Māori speakers also much prefer a passive sentence structure that puts the action first, and often even omits the agent altogether: kua horoia ngā rihi (e au) (have been washed the dishes [by me]). The language itself immerses us in being and doing. Passives soften the language: things happen, rather than I/you/he/they making them happen: 'words were spoken' rather than 'he spoke words'. This language structure has social effects. It expresses social ways of being; passives allow much to be said obliquely without identifying an actor, thereby avoiding direct confrontation, and protecting social collectivity.

This way of speaking illustrates how culture, in all its subtlety, lives in language. I am reminded that, socially, Māori seem naturally to foreground shared states of being and emotion before individuals. This orientation is hard to explain, but it produces the effect of empathy and engagement that I encounter constantly in Māori contexts. Even in our fighting, we were engaging with one another. The Māori word for an enemy or opponent is hoariri, an 'angry friend' – hoa refers to a relationship and riri is 'angry'. Your opponent is someone you respect enough to fight with, to give your attention to, and to even die with. Thus the language reflects the profound *relationality* that has always attracted me to the Māori world, from the first moments in Dannevirke when I met Maria and her friends, and watched the daring Hana girls.

In my Māori language classes I discovered new ways to think about past and future – and the relationship between them. Te wā o mua refers to the 'olden days', or days past. Mua is also a location term for *in front*, for instance, pou mua, front post of the meeting house. In other words, past time is associated with the front: the past is located metaphorically in front of us. We face the past; it is, in a sense, see-able in memory. On the other hand, the future lies behind us. A word for the location 'behind' is muri, which is also a term for the future. The future remains largely unseen (by ordinary people, anyway), and we move into this unknown guided only from where we came. We walk backwards into the future.

It takes only a moment to realise the sensible logic of this thinking, and that Pākehā insistence on 'forgetting the past' becomes possible only if we believe the past is lost behind us, out of sight and gone. If, on the other hand, we recognise that we express, or embody, our origins – and that our knowledge comes from past experience – it is impossible to overlook the past because *it is who we are*. And that past encompasses our genealogical stories that interweave us with all other people, and places, in a web of endless (positive and negative, balancing and unbalancing) relationships. With these, we move constantly from a past to a future.

———

Our first assignment was the self-introduction known as a pepeha, which we had to present to our classmates without notes. We were given a framework: find the river, mountain, and tribe that expressed our links to the land, to our ancestors. A pepeha makes connections and identifies our links with others; it acknowledges that we are a product or even an embodiment of our forebears rather than a being of our own making; it draws our dead close as we meet strangers. For many, a mountain or a river *is* an ancestor, so there is no distinction between the river or mountain and the speaker.

I was puzzled about how a Pākehā might express their identifying place. After class, I asked the teacher about a 'Pākehā pepeha – is it possible?' My question was existential, really, and revealed my individualism, as well as my emerging insights into the meanings of being 'of' a place. My teacher insisted I choose one parent and refer to their homeland's mountain and river. I understood her point. How could I say 'Nō Tāmaki-makau-rau ahau' (I am *from* Tāmaki-makau-rau)? The 'nō' seemed to mean something far more lasting, ancient and complicated than identifying where I was 'from'. In Māori terms it referred to being 'of' a place, which is a very different thing. It was the same with 'ko'. How could I say 'Ko Waitematā te moana' (the Waitematā is the harbour)? For me, the Waitematā is a place I call home, but it is not 'the' body of water that calls into being a tribal and historical identity as for Ngāti Whātua or the Waiohua.

Although I understood that my past carried my present, I was resistant to claiming my English ancestors. I had to face up to the fact that I did not know my 'ancestral' mountain and river – I did not even know my ancestors, and did not particularly want to. I am not an English person, and I did not feel anything for my forebears. I knew little about my orphan mother's origins, so – reluctantly – I researched my father's ancestors, and the ship *Tamaroa* that carried my parents to New Zealand in 1952. I checked Google for a landscape feature my father's predecessors might have seen (strangely, it did not occur to me to ask my father's brother in England). I searched for 'the highest hill in Northumberland' and discovered the not-very-impressive 815-metre high 'The Cheviot', with a mar-vellously spooky description: 'the summit is a desolate-looking tract of treacherous moss-hags and oozy peat-flats, traversed by deep sykes [gullies] and interspersed with black stagnant pools'.[1]

Images of The Cheviot's foreign desolation did not stir me, but I stated 'Ko te Cheviot tōku maunga' (The Cheviot is my mountain) for my pepeha. I then claimed the mighty industrial river Tyne that runs some distance away from The Cheviot through my father's rejected city of Newcastle. 'Ko te Tyne tōku awa' (the Tyne is my river). I had never been to these places and, at best, they were hazy ideas. I recited my pepeha without much conviction, uncertain of its relationship with me, or at least who I understood myself to be.

A surprising whakapapa

As I prepared my pepeha, I did not entirely ignore my mother's side. By now, I had two children, and I had separated from William. My boys were growing up, and they were interested in their grandmother's unexplained origins. I started to do some research. What I discovered was astonishing; it tied me into New Zealand history in a way I could never have imagined.

Completely unbeknown to me, my mother's family had lived in New Zealand in the nineteenth century. All my life, I thought I was a first-generation English immigrant, and I was wrong. My family had been here before, and most of them had returned to England. I was utterly surprised by my revealed whakapapa.

I found that my great-great-grandmother, Janet Buchanan, arrived in New Zealand as a fourteen-year-old girl in 1857 on the *Dinapore*, with her parents and seven brothers and sisters.[1] Her father, Dr Andrew Buchanan, had been born in Jamaica, a son of British sugar-plantation owners. Andrew was among those wealthy nineteenth-century British migrants who saw financial and political opportunities in the new colonies. His 'adventurous propensity' and 'an interest in colonial matters', as he put it in a letter in March 1864, brought him to New Zealand.[2] He arrived with no intention of staying, and quickly acquired property.

Discovering my new-found genealogy was in several respects unsettling – not least in revealing some of my dubious attitudes towards social class. I had always felt a kinship to my mother's side, even though that side of my family had never truly existed for me. By contrast, I felt little connection to my father's working-class ancestors. His anxiously narrow views on knowledge, authority and women had always felt alien. Surely I came from somewhere else – somewhere more expansive, generous, liberal, self-assured, more *upper-class*? Now, on my mother's side, I had located my real origins.

I laughed at the insane logic of these thoughts. I was pleased to have family links to wealth and oppressive power? As a left-wing political champion of the workers and the disadvantaged, I felt sharply cynical about my dismissal of my working-class father's family, and about my direct genealogical connection with the exploitative relationships required for great wealth. And my relations were slave owners.

Then, resentment. My mother's ejection from her birth family had denied me the confidence conferred by privilege; I had been cruelly deprived of a cerebral life and other cultural capital that, I imagined, comes with affluence. I pictured a poised mother giving me interesting books, introducing me to music and literature, having informed conversations with me, taking me to fascinating places to meet clever friends – not the mother I had, who stuttered, lacked intellectual confidence, and was relatively poorly educated. Yes, these, too, were shameful thoughts.

For a while I was sidetracked into the discovery that Andrew was descended from an African slave. His mother, Jane Gowie, a Jamaican-born Scot, was a 'quadroon' – a term for a person one-quarter Black. In 1785, under one of the so-called Private Acts of the Jamaican assembly, Jane Gowie (along with a list of others) was in effect pardoned for her dark origins by being given 'the same rights and privileges with English subjects, born of white parents, under certain restrictions'.[3] So Andrew was born officially 'white', though his great-grandmother's mother, my eight-times-great-grandmother, was African. This direct ancestral link into a global racist history took a while to digest.

I came back to the New Zealand connection, searching eagerly for evidence of my ancestors' engagements with Māori. On board the *Dinapore* was a group of British army officers, arriving from military postings in India. They were to support the British 65th Regiment in the forceful removal of land from Māori tribes – the long and devastating engagement now known as the New Zealand Wars. These men joined the 12,000 British and Irish troops in New Zealand at the time, the largest massing of imperial troops outside of India.[4] Janet's older sisters married two of the officers, who became directly involved in planning attacks in Taranaki and in the Waikato.[5] I did not find out much about those particular distant uncles, except that they fought Māori forced to defend their own territories against the violent and overwhelming incursions of colonising Pākehā who, quite simply, wanted Māori land for themselves.

———

Then I discovered that an even more remote relative was at the signing of the Treaty of Waitangi between hapū leaders and the Crown at Waitangi in the Bay of Islands on 5 and 6 February 1840. My great-grandmother's sister's husband, Charles Robertson, was in the Pākehā crowd at the back of the large tent erected for the signing, and his eyewitness account was published two weeks later in the *Sydney Herald*.[6]

Robertson was in the Bay of Islands to buy land. He was

taking part in the rapacious purchasing of land, known as
'land-sharking', that, he noted in a letter at the time, urgently
needed some political regulation. He joined a group of 'about
100' Pākehā 'at the first sale of allotments' for a planned
township in Kororāreka (now Russell), just over the water from
Waitangi. On behalf of a friend in Sydney, who was excited by
the big profits to be made from New Zealand land speculation,
Robertson bought two plots, for £49 and £29. These, he said,

> in less than twelve months, will be worth some hundreds.
> ... One of my passengers paid down £500 for a lot facing
> the harbour, measuring 50 feet by 80; this patch was
> purchased three years ago for £75, and five years since it
> was obtained for two muskets and a keg of powder. The
> price of land has risen in an extraordinary manner, and
> houses are springing up like mushrooms.[7]

Robertson could see that local Māori leaders were worried
about Pākehā influences on their people. 'The natives,' wrote
Robertson (the term 'Māori' was not yet in common use), 'are
retiring to other parts of the island, as the whites advance. This
is owing to the policy of the chiefs, who see that their power
over their tribes is insignificant if they keep near the white
people; and they have been always accustomed to have the
entire control of those under them.'[8]

The speculators and settlers grumbled about the British
Crown's threat to regulate the chaotic land sales in New
Zealand. It suited them to deal directly with Māori 'land owners'
who were keen to acquire guns and powder. Robertson knew
there was an urgent need for clear legal governance in New
Zealand because, as he put it:

every man [by which he probably meant native and settler alike] does as he likes ... with respect to private agreements, there is no security: a man will actually sign his name to a private agreement, and if it suits his purpose, he will break it to-morrow. ... if ever there was a spot on the globe that required the power of law, it will be required, and I think solicited, by many here ... and the sooner Great Britain or any nation can call themselves masters of New Zealand, the better for all parties; sooner or later, it must take place.[9]

And it very soon did take place. Robertson met William Hobson, the Englishman charged with taking control of the situation. Hobson had come to the Bay of Islands with orders from Sir George Gipps, the Governor of New South Wales, on behalf of the Crown to get Māori leaders to agree that British sovereignty would extend to New Zealand. On the appointed day, Wednesday 5 February 1840, Robertson rowed across the bay from Kororāreka to Waitangi to witness the discussion (it was hardly a negotiation) between hapū leaders and Hobson. 'The sight was very interesting, and would have been the subject of a fine picture to an artist,' he wrote in a letter.

The meeting having assembled within a very large tent, the mingled costume of the Chiefs, some dressed in European clothes, others in their native mats, their animated gestures when addressing and giving their opinion to the new measures, evidently proving a people of great mental capacity.[10]

Many of the chiefs argued that the proposed agreement would disadvantage them. It would make them 'slaves, hewers of wood and drawers of water, and [they would be] driven to break stones on the road'. In particular, reported my ancestor, Tareha of Kororāreka 'worked himself up to a frenzy against it. ... There appeared to be considerable opposition at first to the idea of having a governor over them, but [they agreed] that a governor might come and exercise authority over the Europeans.'[11] In the end, and for reasons that have fuelled historical debate since, the leaders accepted the proposed arrangement. Tareha said that he 'would be satisfied to be guided, as heretofore, by the advice and counsel of Mr Williams and Mr Busby'. James Busby (the British consular representative) and the Reverend Henry Williams (a missionary in Paihia) were the two interpreters who, respectively, helped Hobson draft the wording of the Treaty in English and in te reo Māori.

Two days later, Charles Robertson left the Bay of Islands aboard the *Samuel Winter*, carrying with him Hobson's official dispatches to Gipps that announced 'the first formation of the union between a civilised and savage state by treaty', the 'union of New Zealand with the British Empire'.[12] Little over a year later, Lieutenant-Governor Hobson became Governor of New Zealand, reporting to a government on the other side of the world.

———

My other male ancestors had a significant impact on the fate of Māori simply through their lack of curiosity about the indigenous people who wanted to assert their mana and protect their lands from the insatiable settlers. Andrew Buchanan became a New Zealand politician in 1862.[13] In Dunedin, his daughter Janet married Captain William Baldwin, my great-great-grandfather, a writer and ex-British Army officer who had fought in India's first war of independence ('the Indian

Mutiny'). Baldwin, too, became a politician, a representative
for the Otago goldfields. I looked for evidence of these two
men's engagement with – or even interest in – Māori. Baldwin
did have 'a couple of half-castes' working on Pātearoa Station,
his Central Otago sheep run that was one of the largest wool
exporters in the country – and in the goldfields he encountered
a few of what he in his autobiographical novel referred to as
'Maories that used to work up in Maori Gully'.[14] But, like other
settlers, he expressed – to judge by his writing – little knowledge
of or curiosity about Māori.

Andrew Buchanan had more to say about what he called
'conquering the natives'.[15] He kept a diary for one sitting of the
Legislative Council in Wellington in 1865, during the height
of the New Zealand Wars that had now spread to almost all
areas of the North Island. He seemed at least to tolerate, and
perhaps to approve, the violence with which land acquisition
was proceeding.

> Tuesday 25 July 1865: We dined at the Club ... conversation
> principally about the taking of Wararoa Pah [Wereroa pā]
> which seems to have been accomplished very luckily ... it
> was necessary to take [the pā] before the plan of making a
> road between Taranaki and Wanganui could be carried out.

> Sunday 27 August 1865: It is in the neighbourhood of Hick's
> Bay ... where the colonial forces so gallantly took a pah, and
> bayoneted 25 Maori.[16]

> Thursday 14 September 1865: ... [colonial troops with Māori
> supporters near Ōpōtiki] attacked and destroyed a pah
> and some wharves and killed 11 Hau Haus [resistant Māori],
> without any loss on our part ...[17]

Reading Andrew Buchanan's diaries, I have the sense that my ancestor was a ditherer when it came to 'the Māori question'. At one point he comments that his colleague James FitzGerald, a politician 'unpopular in the House on account of his strong Māori proclivities', could be quite useful because 'he has the confidence of some of the leading rebel chiefs, whose opinions and grievances we want to know, rather than those of the friendly natives'.[18] But this looks simply like tactical curiosity; Buchanan was clearly not in the camp of the so-called 'philo-Maori' politicians who denounced coercive measures against Māori as 'unjust, cruel and impolitic', and the land confiscations as 'sheer robbery'.[19] He almost certainly would have supported the New Zealand Settlements Act 1863, which, directly contrary to the spirit of the Treaty of Waitangi, allowed for confiscation of any Māori land, without compensation, from any North Island tribes who, in defending their lands, were 'in rebellion against Her Majesty's authority'. This resulted in the loss to Māori of millions of acres in Taranaki, Waikato and the Bay of Plenty.[20] Buchanan saw himself as a 'realist' (as he put it): taking land from Māori was simply necessary. He was in the business of colonisation, just as were his sons-in-law, the military officers trained to put down native rebellions. They were people with a job to do: developing the land for productive cultivation and civilising the world. They considered themselves superior to 'the natives' about whom they knew very little.

So there it was: my ancestors had been at the signing of the Treaty of Waitangi, and they had presided as politicians over the betrayal of that Treaty. My tūpuna uncles had a direct relationship with Waikato and Taranaki Māori, fighting them as they protected their territories from Pākehā incursions. I had always accepted that even though I had no direct ancestral link, 'my' people – that is, the British – were the aggressors in the New Zealand Wars. But a real family involvement brought those wars disturbingly close. I had whakapapa that linked me to Māori, through battle and through political force.

I was no longer simply a child of new immigrants living on a land devoid of actual ancestral presence. I had found an embodied nineteenth-century stake in this place. I had feelings that were very mixed but, strangely, largely positive. I felt that, somehow, if I had a claim to our past, I also had a claim to our future.

———

As far as the link to my mother Ruth is concerned, William Baldwin and Janet Buchanan's daughter Olave, my great-grandmother, was born in Dunedin in 1873. She left New Zealand as a young woman, and married William Oswald Story, later a vice-admiral in the British Royal Navy and then the Canadian Navy. One of their many children was Janet Story.

In London in 1928, Janet Story, a well-off widow with two children, became pregnant with my mother. To hide the shame of the illegitimate baby's existence, she put my mother – whom she named Ruth – in a country orphanage. Ruth was not told about her origins.

I learned some of this story from my mother who, in her fifties, finally discovered her mother. That scrap of brown paper, carefully folded in her purse when she travelled to New Zealand as a young wife, carried the name of two girls and a London address. Ruth had found these names when she was twelve years old, on the underside of the wrapping on a parcel addressed to her. She secretly hid that precious scrap of paper because she knew it would one day lead her to her mother.

Thanks to that handwritten London address, after a lot of luck and sleuthing, we found Ruth's mother, and a real person emerged from the ghost we had always lived with. Ruth travelled to London when Janet agreed to meet her there, in a public place in Kew Gardens, on condition that Ruth 'not ask any questions about her origins'. All Janet would allow was superficial chat. One tiny part of a mystery was solved, but Janet refused to acknowledge Ruth as her daughter, so we were none the wiser about Ruth's abandonment. Janet subsequently vanished. Then, in a plot stranger than a detective novel, Ruth finally met Janet again, this time back in New Zealand, not long before Janet died. And we discovered Ruth's half-sister, who had been living in Wellington for more than three decades.

My aunt's name was Monica and I liked her immediately. I began regular visits to Wellington, and we had long conversations about her mother, my grandmother Janet. Monica's stories of her unhappy childhood in England destroyed my fantasies about the advantages of having wealthy parents. She told me that Janet was a socialite, an independent and troubled woman, who showed little emotional warmth for her two legitimate daughters. Ruth was the result of an affair with a married man. Monica, who was ten years old when Ruth was born, knew about Ruth's existence, but nothing else. Janet had later tried at least twice to kill herself. This was a sad story.

My mother met her half-sister. They did not get on well. Monica was upper-class and seemed cool towards my mother, who stuttered anxiously in her presence. Ruth accepted Monica's distance, as though anticipating rejection; I found this strange. I was glad to meet Monica's children, my cousins, but we had little in common. My dreams of a reunion with my long-lost family quickly evaporated.

When my aunt died in 2013, I went to her funeral with my mother – who was by then in her eighties and suffering the onset of dementia. The funeral parlour was full of family and friends; Monica's coffin lay beneath a handsome array of pink and white flowers. Standing one after another, my family members spoke, addressing the mourners. When my mother and I stood to speak, I could not help my tears. The people in this room had haunted us all our lives. For as long as I could remember, I had wondered about whether I had cousins and aunts and uncles, and here they were. Our mother's loss and grief at being abandoned at birth, at being told nothing about her origins, and her feeling of 'belonging to no one', had shaped each of my siblings' emotional lives. I walked to the coffin, put my hand on its shiny closed surface and spoke directly to my aunt. I reminded her about our excitement at finding we had a family.

Addressing her felt natural. For me, it would have felt very strange, and wrong, simply to stand and ignore her, invisibly lying there. Finally, no words in English would do. Saying 'farewell, dear aunt' seemed prosaic somehow; it was in Māori tangihanga that I had learned how to address the dead. The words 'Haere atu rā, tōku whaea kēkē ātaahua, ki ōu mātua tupuna. Moe mai, moe mai rā' came to me (Farewell, my beautiful aunt, go to your ancestors. Sleep well). I was simply expressing my sorrow in a way that felt right.

———

Then, out of the blue, we found Ruth's father, my grandfather. One of his other children, who had known of the mysterious

'Ruth' all her adult life, tracked us down through Facebook.
Robert Alan Bicknell, a wealthy London car dealer, had had five
children with four women, and Ruth was one of them. I now had
more relatives than I could ever have imagined. I met some of
them in England, heard from some in Canada, and visited some
in New Zealand. We had cups of tea together, and I liked many
of them very much, though I was startled when one introduced
me to a friend in an English village as 'an expert on New Zealand
before it was ours'!

For most of my life, everything had stopped at Ruth. Now,
a past was opening up, longer, larger and more surprising
than I could have imagined. I had dreamt of a family, and the
ghosts had become real. I now had a huge crowd of relations.
But, like a tree having grown on an open plain, I found myself
uncomfortable in a forest. And Ruth was losing her memory;
it was too late for her to enjoy the family relationships she had
missed all her life.

———

All this altered my pepeha; it changed who I felt myself to be.
My teacher at the wānanga had said that the pepeha not only
introduced the speaker, but ideally made ancestral links with
the listeners. I had now found a very real link to Māori.

In my new pepeha, I claimed my ancestors' presence here.
Instead of naming the *Tamaroa* in 1952 as my originary mode of
arrival as required by the pepeha format, I claimed the *Dinapore*
in 1857. I named the hill outside my mother's maternity ward.
I could not call Maungakiekie 'my' mountain, tōku maunga, in
the way it is claimed by the people of Ngāti Whātua. But I could
claim it as the mountain that watched over my emergence into

the world: 'I whānau mai ahau i te taha o Maungakiekie.' (I was born beside Maungakiekie.)

Another phrase of my pepeha now felt richer: 'He Pākehā ahau' (I am a Pākehā). This word kept deepening with my sense of myself and the Māori relationships that shaped me, in all their complexities. As a Pākehā, I claimed the brutal colonising forces as well as the loyal friendships that had become so dear to me. All of those energetic engagements haunted each other in dogged counterpoint. I could not escape the contradictions, those doubled elements, and nor did I want to. They made me who I was.

Risky territory

The woman in my feminist theory class had a wide, open face, and an intense curiosity. She seemed devoid of the self-consciousness that so often persuades students to hide their thoughts. She was older than the others – and at least ten years older than me, her lecturer – and she seemed to delight at finding herself in a university classroom. She had the enthusiastic and generous manner of a benevolent school-teacher, and I warmed to her immediately. She introduced herself as Kuni Jenkins, from Ngāti Porou. She was, indeed, a primary school teacher, with three adult daughters, and, aiming for a principalship, had returned to university to do postgraduate research.

She explained her unusual name. Her father had taken one look at his newborn daughter's snub nose and declared her his little kunekune pig, and the nickname Kuni stuck. I smiled at her story, and she grinned back.

It was the late 1980s and by now I had gained a doctorate, and an academic position, at the University of Auckland. I was discovering the greatest joy of being a lecturer: the students in my classrooms. Many would become my friends, and Kuni would become like a mother to me. She was the wise, available, smart, accepting woman I had wanted my own mother to be. Eventually she would guide me in a Māori world that would preoccupy me for the rest of my life.

Kuni spoke her mind plainly, often with piercing clarity, but sometimes at such an oblique angle I was unsure of her meaning.

She did well as a student – she was fearlessly original in her thinking, and she enjoyed writing. We had an affectionate relationship, so it was no surprise when she asked me to supervise her doctoral thesis.

I was struck by the clarity of her research question – and more struck by the fact that it would never have occurred to me. What, she wondered, was the Māori involvement in the establishment of the first school in New Zealand? I had assumed, without thinking about it, that the story of New Zealand schools was a European one: that colonists set up English-language schools in Pākehā towns and required (by law) the attendance of Māori children, who subsequently lost their language. This did happen, but it was by no means the only narrative about Māori in New Zealand schools. A far more fascinating story was to be found in the Māori establishment of New Zealand's first school in the early nineteenth century, and that was the story that interested Kuni.

My new doctoral student approached all her research work as a Māori person; she did not default, in the way that came naturally to me, to the Pākehā point of view and she never took the Pākehā written histories at face value. But nor did she ignore the Pākehā accounts, which is sometimes the practice among Māori students. She read Pākehā historians with enthusiasm, always looking for the Māori story hidden in the Pākehā one. She read *through* the texts, seeing into their Māori shadows, forming solid new insights from the ghostly figures found there.

We became a tight team of two: Kuni enjoyed my pushing her thinking, my encouragement and excitement; I loved her approach to reading the archives. I asked her once whether learning gave her the feeling that I had of neurons growing. Discovering something startlingly new seemed to generate a physical sensation in my brain – a sharp, pleasurable prickle of absolute attention, and a sudden sense of the world changing.

One of these moments that remains a vivid memory occurred after Kuni and I had both read a Pākehā eyewitness account of what has long been remembered as 'the first sermon in New Zealand'.[1] It had taken place a couple of days after the 1814 arrival at Rangihoua in the Bay of Islands of the first permanent Pākehā settlers. The Yorkshireman Samuel Marsden, an Anglican missionary and prominent landowner living in Australia, had been invited by Māori visiting Sydney to send a schoolteacher to the northern Bay of Islands to teach the children of the hapū to read and write (in Māori). It was Christmas Day, and the Reverend Marsden, on the beach at Rangihoua, read a public sermon for the Christmas Day service, including St Luke's passage about the birth of the baby Jesus.

Marsden did not speak Māori with any fluency. Ruatara, the man who had invited the settlers, was to be the translator. The assumption is that Ruatara rendered Marsden's words into te reo Māori for the four hundred or so Māori at the event. Hence, the first sermon was preached on New Zealand soil.

Kuni and I were discussing this scene, sitting together at a friend's table after lunch, having exchanged amused glances about that fussy piece of cutlery, the butter knife. To fill in a silence, I commented on how strange it must have been to Māori, hearing about Jesus. Kuni said calmly, with her signature opacity: 'It didn't happen.' 'What didn't?' I asked. 'The sermon,' she replied, wielding the butter knife. 'It didn't happen.'

I was puzzled. Was this another of her obscure remarks? But the explanation, when it came, was self-evident: there by the beach at Rangihoua on that day, none of the Māori present, except Ruatara, understood much English. What Ruatara

actually said is not recorded but, Kuni argued, he would not
have simply translated St Luke's words in which the angel
announced to the shepherds the birth of Christ ('I bring you
good tidings of great joy, which shall be to all people. For unto
you is born this day in the city of David a Saviour, which is Christ
the Lord'), or told the curious and impatient crowd about
an irrelevant Pākehā baby born in a land that none of them
had ever heard of. Rather, Ruatara would have had entirely
different business in mind that day: explaining who these newly
arrived Pākehā strangers were, why he had invited them to live
permanently amongst the hapū, and why they were to be both
trusted and protected. He may have tried to explain something
of the Pākehā god to the people. But none of the Māori listeners
encountered a *sermon*. So, Kuni announced dramatically, in the
Māori world, there was no sermon!

This insight was an awakening, a moment when my
perspective shifted irrevocably. Kuni was not making an arcane
semantic point. Her view of the non-sermon pulled a Māori
viewpoint into focus, at the same time making me conscious
of my default Pākehā patterns of attention. What the listening
people heard was not Marsden's sermon, but an incomprehen-
sible Pākehā whaikōrero. In effect, they did not 'hear' Marsden;
they heard only the kōrero of Ruatara, their relation. He was the
one people called out to, asking questions.

The English newcomers may have thought Christianity had
arrived – indeed, 'the first Christmas' and 'the first sermon' is a
moment still celebrated (including by Māori). But for Māori at
Rangihoua at that time, the unknown and alien Christian God
was still in England – and maybe on the ship that had brought
these Pākehā and their astonishing array of goods. The people
would have expected the Pākehā to have their own gods, but

these gods were not of the Māori world, te ao Māori. The idea
that a Pākehā god might rule over all the forces in the Māori
world would have been preposterous.

Thus began my training: thinking as a Pākehā informed by a
Māori point of view. My student had become my teacher. From
then on, I tried to look, as Kuni looked, *through* the archival
accounts of the earliest settlers' lived experience amongst
Māori, opening my attention first and foremost to possible
Māori interpretations. This new pattern of attention required
that I learn about what Māori interpretations might be. I read
Māori writers and listened hungrily to Māori speakers, slowly
but surely gaining a new sense of the Māori world.

It occurred to me that I was learning, finally, to think like
a proper Pākehā. If Pākehā people exist in terms of our relationship with Māori, then we have to be able to think with a
Māori-informed point of view. How else can the relationship
work? However imperfect or limited our Pākehā perceptions
might be, to *be* Pākehā, to fully inhabit that identity, is to be
permanently oriented to Māori, as well as to know about our
historical entanglements. If 'Pākehā thinking' has a reflexive
openness to Māori, then it is quite different from European
thinking. It is peculiarly located here, with Māori. And once you
'get' that, you can no longer 'un-get' it. I see this as similar to the
idea that the thing, once seen, can never again be unseen, just
as Buddhist teaching changes for ever your perception of the
sanctity of life even if you stop accepting Buddhist teachings.

This is not to suggest that all Māori think alike, and that
there is one 'Māori point of view'. In fact, I now noticed the
political and analytical differences amongst my Māori friends
and acquaintances. But Māori seem to have some pervasive
shared ways of being, and it was these that I was absorbing.

I was not merely learning through my ears and eyes, but also through my skin, the hairs on the back of my neck, the pressure of air in a room.[2] Who cannot feel a connection with a stranger through a lengthened hongi – the intake of breath and the press of the forehead, the grasp of a strong hand? My openness to Māori meant an awareness of the many complexities of Māori thought, and an ability to sit with those differences, just as my friends did.

It is true to say that Kuni was being criticised by some quite powerful Māori scholars for her work with me, a Pākehā – why not put energy into other Māori rather than a Pākehā? And why should a Pākehā be writing about Māori history? We were both aware of the criticisms, but Kuni was clear that there was an audience for our shared work; together we produced something valuable that was, she believed, worth giving attention to.

———

Kuni and I enjoyed our engagement so much that we decided to write a book on the earliest Māori interest in reading and writing, and the establishment of the first school in New Zealand. Our approach, we agreed, was original enough to warrant being published. We travelled to the north to talk to Ngāpuhi and the people who now had mana whenua in the sites of schooling's beginnings. We made it clear that we were not writing about Māori forms of education, such as the traditional systems of wānanga. We were interested in the peculiar European cultural tradition of the *school*, with its focus on reading and writing, and sitting in rows listening to a teacher – a pattern of teaching and learning developed in Europe from the pedagogy of the Christian churches.

At first, we were treated warily. Kuni was from a different
tribal region, Ngāti Porou, once attacked by the musket-rich
Ngāpuhi in a dark period still remembered by both sides. I
was a Pākehā and largely unknown. I think it was simpler for
me. Having no pre-existing relationships with Ngāpuhi, I was
easier to dismiss, ignore or talk to. Kuni and I were very aware
that Māori tended to be suspicious of researchers' approaches.
As the Tūhoe rangatira John Rangihau, advising the Pākehā
researcher Michael King, once put it, 'If [a Māori] disapproves
of a project, he does nothing; if he approves, he opens doors,
points you in the right direction, then leaves it to you.'[3]

Bit by bit, doors were opened. With support from a research
grant, Kuni and I drove from place to distant place, looking
at the land on which our history took place, and talking with
anyone who showed interest in our project. I was always the
driver, because I like driving, and I chose our stopping places
because I am bossy. Kuni would have been happy to eat at a
burger joint or stay at a downmarket motel. But I would be on
the lookout for a nice restaurant and comfortable accommodation. 'Let's stay here,' I'd say, sweeping up a tree-lined driveway.
'If we have to,' she'd reply, dryly. Then we would often have to
share a room, and sometimes even a large bed, to save money.
I enjoyed her laconic wit, and she tolerated my fussiness, and
laughed at my big-city pretensions.

———

It was not particularly easy to explain how my sense of myself
was changing. It all seemed so subtle, so personal. When I spoke
to Pākehā audiences about this research, I would sometimes be
quizzed about working as a Pākehā in a Māori situation; I heard

stories about how difficult it was to ensure meetings, get responses to emails and so on. All I could do was listen. I was unsure what my questioners wanted from me – was it a checklist of 'how to work with Māori'? I could not explain what motivated me, or what made my relationships with Māori 'work', or not. Sometimes, it all seemed to boil down to an involuntary feeling – warm, alert, humorous – rather than anything I could rationally discuss.

I was forced to be a bit more explicit one uncomfortable summer's day at a conference in Australia. I was wearing a beautiful speckled piece of pounamu, a gift from Kuni. It is a very self-effacing piece of greenstone, flat and round, unpolished, with a small hole through which is tied a black string. It hangs around my neck, just heavy enough to let me know it is there. It is smooth, solidly comforting, swirled light and dark like a deep green pool, and it warms itself against my skin. This taonga pounamu is far more to me than a decoration; it ties me to Kuni and our work together, and to Aotearoa New Zealand. It feels part of me, almost alive in our relationship.

At the Brisbane conference, the greenstone attracted some unanticipated attention. I had been invited to speak about early-nineteenth-century Māori interest in schools in Australia. A group of academics, we sat in a cool air-conditioned room, as the gum trees outside glittered in light as hard as glass. It was almost lunchtime, and things were winding up. As white liberal educators concerned about Aboriginal education, the group's concluding comments were likely, I knew, to run a certain course. And so they did, from the self-critical 'It's all right for us sitting here all comfortable; who is out there getting their hands dirty amongst the local indigenous groups?' to the anxious 'It is so difficult to work with such poor, remote communities' to the hopeless 'We will make no progress with this government in power, they don't give a shit.' Someone remarked that 'New Zealanders have done much better with their indigenous education'. I was not drawn to respond; I had learned enough not to make any easy comparisons.

Then I felt a sudden tension in the room. A young man aimed a clear shot at me: 'Don't you feel like a deek,' he asked, in his Aussie twang, 'wearing a greenstone round your neck?' He went on. 'That's a Māori thing, isn't it, to wear a greenstone?' His tone was challenging now, and I could read between its lines: I was appropriating something that was not mine, mimicking Māori culture: 'Don't you feel like an eediot? Like a pretentious wally?'

I have always enjoyed the bluntness of my Australian friends, in stark contrast to the oblique diffidence of New Zealanders. But this was not so much blunt as sharp. The room went quiet. The others, sitting in a circle on plastic and chrome chairs, waited for my reply as to whether I was, in fact, a deek.

My hand automatically grasped the blameless pounamu. I explained that I was not *trying* to be anything, that the stone was part of me, that it was a beautiful object with its own power and identity, and that it is a companion, linking me to a specific Māori friend as well as embodying some essence of my country. But suddenly all this seemed impossibly – yes – pretentious in a place where such talk is seen either as stupidly mystical or usurping someone else's culture.

My interlocutor would not let it go. 'Māori wear greenstone, so isn't it cultural appropriation when white people do it? I wouldn't paint my body like Aboriginal Australians do ... aren't you trying to be something you are not?'

I took a breath and did my best. 'I take your point,' I said. 'I, too, bristle at non-indigenous people in "native dress". But an act of cultural appropriation, surely, is made without a real relationship, without permission. A pounamu is gifted, rather than purchased as a decoration. This stone is a gift from my friend Kuni. For Māori, a gift embodies a reciprocity. That gift is a statement of our mutual relationship, and a symbol of my loyal engagement with Māori.' I added for good measure: 'I am not trying to be a Māori. I am a Pākehā and this stone, for me, expresses that identity.'

Afterwards, a young woman approached me: 'I'm jealous of you. We white Australians don't have anything like a greenstone to say who we are.' I tried not to feel a bit of (unwarranted) pride as a Pākehā New Zealander. But my position was not – and is not – a confident one. I rely on my Māori friends to allow me to wear the pounamu. If they told me I was 'a dick', I would not wear one, because I wear it only in relation to them. I might instead have pāua-shell earrings or a pōhutukawa flower brooch to represent my New Zealand-ness. But these objects would not hold a relationship with my Māori friends as my warm greenstone does, in the heft of the small solid stone.

———

More challenging questions were to come. With her PhD nearly completed, Kuni had successfully applied for an academic position in my department, and we had become colleagues. We agreed in 1998 to teach my existing feminist theory course together, and we hit on the idea of altering the pedagogy in a radical way.

We had been talking about how to get the Māori students buzzing. Kuni suggested that we divide the course into two streams, each teaching one stream. In one group would be the Māori students and, for practical purposes, the Pacific students; the rest would make up the other stream. At mid-year, Kuni and I would swap streams, so that everyone experienced both teachers and the full curriculum. The course seemed to go well. Assessment included a critique of this teaching experiment – and the student feedback was both interesting and surprising.

Almost uniformly, the Māori and Pacific students loved the course structure, saying things like 'the focus on my culture broadened my horizons to question, argue and debate ... I am sure that it would not have been the same in a class with Pākehā women', and 'the different streams allow Māori and Pacific Island women to identify issues of feminism amongst [our] own ... [usually] the discussions are taken over by Pākehā women'.

By contrast, many of the Pākehā students complained of feeling cheated: 'Nothing can change unless we know what needs to be changed. Behind closed doors doesn't help the process of change'; and 'It does not seem right. Could we not learn from each other? Wouldn't it be valuable to share our differences in experiences?'[4] One seemed so angry about 'imposed separatism' that we worried she would complain to the university authorities or go to the media. As university teachers taking some risks in academic practice, Kuni and I were on uncertain ground.

The students' responses raised a thorny question. Did these incompatible reactions suggest big problems for so-called cross-cultural dialogue? What if dialogue is not of much interest, or much use, to one side of the proposed conversation? The Māori students did not need to hear from their Pākehā peers. The Pākehā world was not a strange place to them. And why should Māori have to spend effort listening to or teaching their classmates to produce a satisfying dialogue for them? It seemed that the Pākehā students wanted direct access to the Māori and Pacific women's emotional and experiential lives, to their thoughts, feelings and cultures. It did not pass my notice that this was an echo of the perennial imperialist desire 'Let me on to your territory', with its extractive logic 'Let me mine you for my discoveries.' They wanted Māori attention: 'Teach me! I need you to save me from what I do not know!' They wanted to be understood, not challenged, by Māori.

The Pākehā students' reactions forced me to interrogate my own position. I had by then worked alongside Māori over a long period, and had read widely, so I did not share that almost indignant need to 'access' Māori. However, I did understand the Pākehā wish for redemptive attention from Māori.

The desire for redemption is a powerful human urge. In our simple stories of goodies and baddies in New Zealand history, both Māori and liberal Pākehā tend to locate us Pākehā on the shameful baddie side. For some, positive Māori attention can help us feel rescued from that position. When Māori turn away from us, we feel awful, even angry. We worry that they do not like us, and that we – at some level – deserve their condemnation. Their responsiveness would make us feel better. Given their attention, we would feel forgiven for our colonial history and our cultural dominance which, after all, is not the fault of present-day individuals. At the same time, our neediness in this regard is humiliating, so we sometimes resent Māori for making us feel this way. A Pākehā need for recognition that we are not 'all bad' in our history is not something we can or should require from Māori; it is work Pākehā need to do for ourselves. Understanding the details of our history is a good place to start.

I remain surprised at the apparently inexhaustible generosity of Māori attention to Pākehā, in the light of their history. Over two hundred years, Māori have been disappointed, disadvantaged and even abused when giving Pākehā their positive regard and trust. Māori had faith that the New Zealand government would protect them with its ideas of equality, as promised by the Treaty of Waitangi. They participated in the nation state, working hard and paying taxes, and even fighting in foreign wars, but they still became impoverished and subordinated. Yet Māori generally maintain an attitude of generosity.

Only one of our Māori students expressed no sympathy for her Pākehā classmates' confusion at our divided course, blurting out: 'Serves them right! Now they know what it is like not having it all your own way!' The more typical reaction was to worry about their peers' hurt. This reaction was in accord with my usual experience, that my Māori acquaintances express deeply felt cultural ideals of care, upholding others' mana (manaaki), and showing a responsibility towards others, the process called whakawhanaungatanga. Even quite unlikeable, or disliked, non-Māori visitors to a Māori setting will experience a welcome – 'kia ora!', have songs sung for them, and receive invitations to share food.

'Being Māori', in a sense, requires expressions of kindness and generosity. My Māori students' concern for their Pākehā classmates seemed natural to them. I felt grateful for their graciousness even though, being crabby and impatient, I often do not display such generosity towards my fellow Pākehā.

When I am with Pākehā, I am often struck by how culturally different we are from Māori. A random moment illustrates this. I had been invited to speak to a (Pākehā) community group about my research. Arriving at the appointed time, I stood at the back of the room, waiting until the previous speaker had finished. No one noticed me there. Eventually, my host came over to greet me. How utterly different this was from arriving at a non-formal Māori event. There, someone would be charged with looking out for the anticipated guest, who is immediately welcomed and offered food or drink. I imagine how a Māori person must feel entering a Pākehā gathering unnoticed, as I was, how cold and alienating that must feel. I have learned from experience that Māori put a lot of store by greetings; in every situation, every arrival is acknowledged. Pākehā will often enter a meeting or a room of people and greet only one or two others, or none of them; for Māori, the warm greeting of each person at a gathering, whether they are already known or not, eases any subsequent interaction.

So it is too with departures. When I leave early from a Pākehā gathering, it is perfectly acceptable to slip away, maybe saying goodbye to one or two. My cultural tendency is to 'not bother the group'. All that greeting and departing takes time and energy and draws attention to oneself. But to sneak off from a Māori gathering can be considered rather odd, offhand or even rude. Acknowledging others is not understood as drawing attention to oneself – quite the opposite. A cheerful goodbye to each person, or the whole group, acknowledges them and our shared place in the web of relationships that hold us together until next time. I once felt obliged to laughingly apologise to a Māori friend for leaving a meeting without saying goodbye: 'I'm a Pākehā, and we can behave strangely at times.'

For Māori, generally speaking, everything is better done with other people, whether it is going to the gym, having lunch, sitting in a meeting, travelling, or visiting. This natural pleasure in collective activity pushes against my love of solitude, and my desire for control over my situation. I notice this, often, in my daily life. Sometimes I go with the group, other times I do not, and these decisions are never easy.

A broken hill

I had not expected it, but my reading and thinking about
Māori–Pākehā relationships altered for me the New Zealand
landscape almost as much as McCahon had. The valleys
and hills and farms of the countryside, and the towns' and
cities' streets and parks, morphed into something new – now
often a source of discomfort as much as aesthetic pleasure.
My increasing knowledge about our shared history steadily
transformed my gaze; the land would never look the same again.

In 2015 I was regularly travelling south from my home in
Auckland to the city of Hamilton, to visit my elderly mother.
After an active middle age during which Ruth had run small
businesses, published her autobiography, and been a personal
assistant to CEOs, she had developed dementia and she now
lived in care, near my sister. The narrow two-lane main road,
State Highway 1, took travellers alongside the huge slow-flowing
Waikato River, through a series of rural towns including one
signposted as Rangiriri. At this point (before the motorway
was constructed), the road was cut through a low hill, before
opening out on to the wide expanse of flat, peaty, Waikato farm
country. Rangiriri is not the sort of place you'd stop. A large,
rather faded nineteenth-century pub and a rural garage were
its only apparent buildings.

I had noticed the road sign saying 'Historic Site', and I knew,
vaguely, that Rangiriri was the location of a famous battle of
the New Zealand Wars in the 1860s. I'd never been keen to visit

historic sites; they were for tourists, and stopping at them merely hindered a swift passage to my destination. And old battle sites, I imagined, were likely to be just empty paddocks.

One weekend, just for a look, I turned off the road at the sign. Only a few dozen metres off the main road was a parking area, with steps up onto the rise through which I had accelerated fortnightly for three years. I read the explanatory board. I could hardly believe it. This small hill was the point of resistance, the fortified pā from which the Waikato people had been defending their land against the incursions of the settlers. I had been driving *right through* the pā. I stood and looked down at the busiest highway in the country, where the oblivious traffic hurtled north and south through the cutting.

I understood then that the highway to Hamilton was in fact a military road, the actual path that armed militia and imperial soldiers – including my British army officer great-uncles – had forced through into the Waikato region in 1863. A large contingent of Māori leaders and warriors from the area had attempted to halt the massive military push from Auckland down into the Waikato, and the seizing of tribal lands for Pākehā settlement. They had been defeated at Rangiriri with 180 Māori taken prisoner, and at least 50 killed. (The treacherous manner of the defeat is well documented by historian Vincent O'Malley.)[1] Now every drive that I had to make through the pā felt like a repeated act of careless disdain for the Māori people who were defending their homelands and their livelihoods.[2] (A wide motorway now skirts around the raised hill, closer to the Waikato River, and several pou stand proudly on the slopes of the old fortifications, marking the heroic defence.

Such stories can be found almost anywhere in New Zealand. I can't glimpse the majestic slopes of Mt Taranaki without

remembering the plight of the Taranaki people who, in 1881, sat
in peaceful opposition to what they called 'te riri Pākehā' – the
white man's anger. The village at Parihaka was destroyed, their
leaders imprisoned and their land sold to settlers. And when I
play on a sandy beach by the peaceful Manukau Harbour with
my grandson, I recall the day in 1864 when two gunboats arrived
at the Manukau Heads. Soldiers disembarked under orders to
destroy every canoe they could find – using explosives to wreck
magnificent carved waka and small transport waka on the
beaches. Land was confiscated, horses and cattle seized and
houses burned. All because the government determined the
Manukau people to be rebels, due to their whakapapa relationships with the Waikato people.[3]

Indeed, the area between Auckland and Hamilton is soaked
in stories of enforced expulsion of peaceful communities of
Māori from their own lands – all called 'rebels' simply for being
related to tribes who resisted invasion by the troops. I came
across this eyewitness description, written by John Featon
in 1879, sixteen years after the British troops' attacks on the
Waikato. With these words, the little town of Tūākau – not
far off the main highway between Auckland and Hamilton – is
transformed:

> The village was situated on the edge of the river, and justly
> considered one of the prettiest and most flourishing in the
> lower Waikato. The land was good; potatoes, kumeras, and
> corn grew luxuriantly, and each year filled the storehouses
> of the natives to overflowing. A water mill close by ground
> their wheat into flour, and their fruit trees were loaded
> with apples and peaches, whilst the branches of the
> vine bending under their juicy weight trailed in the swift

running stream. No wonder the natives were loth to leave
their beloved home. The 65th [imperial troops][emerged]
suddenly from the bush in the rear of the settlement,
and surprised the natives, who, hastily collecting their
[household possessions], moved mournfully down to their
canoes, and with many tears and deep sighs paddled away.[4]

The Auckland airport is located on rich fishing grounds,
with prohibitions on access to the waters around the airport
preventing local Māori from reaching their fishing areas that
are, in any case, polluted. On and on it goes. And place names!
My Tauranga school was on Cameron Road – a main road into
the city in those days. The name Cameron celebrates the man
whose life's great work, according to James Belich, was 'to
attempt to destroy Māori independence'.[5] British Army Lieu-
tenant-General Duncan Cameron led the military invasion of
the Waikato, forcibly taking from Māori the best agricultural
land in New Zealand.

The whole colonised world is like this, a series of
monuments to colonial victors. What bothers me is not so much
the naming, or even the monuments. Most troubling is our
collective wilful amnesia; we do not know who Cameron was,
or what happened at Rangiriri, or Tūākau, or a hundred other
points along a river, up a valley, on a plain or a mountain. Unless
we seek them out, our histories (and particularly the Māori part
of those histories) remain unremembered by the majority of the
New Zealand population. How can we Pākehā understand, let
alone face, Māori anger, if we recognise nothing of its origins?

I started reading obsessively about the places I loved so
much. It was not hard to find the well-researched reports of
the Waitangi Tribunal, and the books by Māori writers like
Patricia Grace, Atholl Anderson and Witi Ihimaera, and Pākehā

writers such as Judith Binney, James Belich, Anne Salmond and Vincent O'Malley. In a mad tumble of reading and seeing, every landscape changed for me. So now, wherever I travel, the violent and often unjust colonial history speaks from the gentle hills, the mountains, the river bends and the grassy paddocks, once bush, now drained and farmed. It is sometimes hard not to feel visceral sadness mixed in with keen curiosity.

———

Once, just to explore a new place, I drove with my sister through the Rūātoki valley south of Whakatāne, into the country of the Ngāi Tūhoe people. We followed the sealed road up the Whakatāne River, crossing (unknowingly) the hated 'confiscation line' – the arbitrary line drawn in 1866 by Pākehā surveyors to mark the government's confiscation of most of the Bay of Plenty, including about half of Tūhoe's best land (even though Tūhoe had not resisted the troops moving into the Waikato, the ostensible reason for the confiscation). We passed kids riding bareback on their horses, barking dogs and chooks squabbling on the roadside. We admired the looming beauty of the hills and their dark forested flanks. Country people always like to know who is coming and going, and we met curious stares as we drove up the narrow country road. But there was hostility in their faces, and no welcome here. One small boy, sitting on an abandoned car, faced us with fierce eyes and defiant tongue, an eloquent pūkana.

I knew that we should not be there, gawking. I turned my little Toyota in a muddy gateway, and turned towards the north, back over the confiscation boundary into the stolen land now owned by Pākehā farmers. When I told some of my Ngāti Porou friends, they laughed at my stupidity in venturing into someone else's territory: typical Pākehā, thinking she can go wherever she wants, expecting a smile and a wave! *They* wouldn't go down there.

I was forced to think about territory, and the way we Pākehā love to 'explore the backblocks' or 'go for a drive in the country', without thinking anything of it. If there is a public road, we'll drive down it to have a look, quite within our rights. Having forced roads through other people's lands, we just assume we can travel uninvited anywhere on an innocent whim, enjoying the scenery, and waving – in our famously friendly way – at the people who live near the road. It's ignorance of our history that allows us to behave like this.

———

It might be more than mere ignorance, too. There is a kind of cultural reflex that allows us Europeans with imperialist instincts to expect that we can travel anywhere, know anything, if we want. Our science is built on the belief that we can and should be able to know everything about the world and the universe; we can and should probe all our human abilities, we should go everywhere – whether Rūātoki or Mars – in this quest. Yet for Māori, and many other indigenous peoples, this right to know is not at all taken for granted. In fact, some knowledge is sacred, shared selectively for particular reasons. Land, too, has its own mana, its own sacredness; land is not simply there for purchase, occupation or exploration.

I saw this first, with sudden clarity, when reading the diaries of Samuel Marsden. After settling his people in the Bay of Islands under the protection of Ruatara, and before he returned to Australia in early 1815, Marsden purchased about 200 acres at Hohi for the Church Missionary Society. A parchment deed, carried from Sydney with Marsden for the purpose, was signed. Twelve axes were handed over. But bitter complaints came quickly. A number of observers, rival chiefs from hapū elsewhere in the Bay, remonstrated. Ngāpuhi would benefit unfairly from having the Pākehā; the blacksmith shop already established on the beach would ensure their hosts would become more powerful. Marsden kindly reassured the worried leaders that they were welcome on the mission land at any time, to trade or to visit.[6]

I sometimes stop at this point when recounting the story. Pākehā listeners are usually satisfied with Marsden's sensible and generous approach. But Māori audiences quickly spot a problem. In 1815, the rival chiefs visiting Hohi had left the land purchase event shaking their heads in anger and frustration. The land, as they knew, had been offered to the Pākehā to live on (the axes sealed the agreement). But, they also knew that land could not be so easily alienated from its people (that is, they did not have a concept of land *ownership*); Hohi was still the territory of their powerful Ngāpuhi rivals. So they could not come casually to visit Ngāpuhi's Pākehā to trade unless Ngāpuhi agreed. And why would the keepers of the Pākehā allow their enemies to benefit from their fruitful acquisition? No doubt Marsden left the country satisfied with this arrangement. His own assumptions about land ownership and purchase, for him, created the whole world.

I like this story because it so neatly illustrates opposing Pākehā and Māori beliefs about land ownership, and the idea of mana whenua, which these days refers to the people who hold the authority *of* the land rather than *over* the land. And it reminds me to beware of my own assumptions. In the Rūātoki valley, I was on the territory of the Tūhoe people, whether or not my ancestors – and all citizens of New Zealand since – 'owned' the public road, and designated surrounding park areas. And why should the Tūhoe people welcome my presence? Not only was I, as a Pākehā, linked directly to brutal land loss, but I was there only to *take* something: visual memories of that remote and beautiful place, snapshots for a personal album.

———

It was in neighbouring Te Arawa country that my father was killed, on a clear October day in 1982. A hard morning sun reflected off the sea along the Matatā coast, the green seaside hills were bright and cheerful, the sky an intense spring blue. Manny, aged thirty, was travelling in his sturdy work vehicle towards the east – I do not know what he set out to do that Sunday. Coming towards him, in his tiny scarlet Morris Mini Minor, was my father, driving a friend to see her husband in Waikato Hospital. As Manny took the corner after the Ōtamarākau railway bridge, he looked down at his radio dials. The sunlight splintered into a thousand fragments, in an instant, metal entered flesh and bone. The larger vehicle had crossed the centre line, crushing the Mini and killing its occupants.

Manny was not injured. This was his first offence, and he ended up doing some community service. We did not go to the court case. We could see no point. Dad was dead. He was only fifty-three.

Manny's family, I discovered later, came from the valley to the west of Rūātoki. His family lived along another colonial line, a road that had been made to link the Armed Constabulary policing posts spread along the western borders of Tūhoe to allow the governing officials to better control the Tūhoe people during the unrest of the 1860s New Zealand Wars. I never knew what became of Manny, but I found his death notice in a newspaper in 2010.

That fatal collision, in a sense, linked our family to a Ngāi Tūhoe family – but as neither family sought the other out, nothing came of our tragic connection.

———

My work as a lecturer and researcher at the university carried on. It was the late 1990s. One day, a meeting was called unexpectedly by one of my Māori colleagues, Graham Smith. Graham was a skilled political strategist who had once sat in my undergraduate sociology of education courses, intrigued by structuralism and critical theory, and he was now a colleague and friend. Our academic group was made up of educational sociologists like myself, educational historians and educational philosophers, including a number of Māori scholars. We were to meet in a part of the university, Old Government House, upstairs, in one of the large meeting rooms.

Autumn sun streamed through the high windows, and I could see out on to a large fir tree, planted more than a hundred years ago by a Governor's gardener, now growing on a lean, but still looking solid and stable. The comfortable chairs did nothing to reduce the tension in the large carpeted room; many of us, including me, had no idea what was coming. This was, compared to today's meetings, a plain, unadorned affair. Now, there are karakia and greetings in Māori to begin, particularly in a meeting called by Māori. Things were done differently in those days.

This spacious building had been the seat of government in New Zealand and a residence of the Governor from the year after the Treaty of Waitangi was signed until government shifted to Wellington in 1865. Its external wood planks were carved to resemble stonemasonry, as though by mimicry the kauri structure, looking like stone, could express the solidity of a colonial government.

In these plush rooms, Governor George Grey lived and ruled over New Zealand during the mid-nineteenth century. Grey was behind the invasion of the Waikato, and presided over the 1860s confiscations. Māori, out of necessity and a natural respect for powerful leaders, kept relationships going with Grey. During his rule, Māori had regularly sat in the corridors of the house, waiting to petition Grey for help with land-hungry settlers, or dishonest government officials, or other Māori who traded or acted unfairly.

At our meeting, Graham got quickly to the point. He and his Māori colleagues were going to shift to the Māori Studies buildings, and call themselves Māori Education. They would no longer be a part of Critical and Philosophical Studies in Education, and would not be occupying offices alongside the rest of us. For a brief moment, I thought I would be shifting and was pleased: Māori Studies had better, more modern offices than ours, on the beautiful marae with its green grass ātea and its welcoming wharenui. Then it struck me: Graham had stated that only Māori staff would be moving. The 'us' did not include me.

I was still looking out of the window – like a child, thinking that if I looked away I would *be* away. The fir tree seemed now on a dangerous lean; it made no sense that it was still standing.

Graham continued: 'We have nothing against our Education colleagues; we have learned a lot from you. But we want to work more closely with our colleagues in Māori Studies, next to our wharenui. We will be moving next week.' He went on about the logistics. I looked at Kuni, my closest friend in the room. Her eyes were cast downwards. I think she already knew. I would not normally leave a room in the middle of a speech, but I found myself walking towards the nearest door, quietly, blindly, barely knowing why, or where, I was going. The cold pale lino floor and thickly painted tongue-and-groove walls were indifferent to my distress; I pushed open a bathroom door and sat glumly on a toilet seat.

Deep sorrow rose in me, and I just had to wait it out. My reaction would remain private. I recalled my students' resistance to being separated from their Māori peers in my class, and my vague impatience with their complaints. Of course my Māori friends should consolidate their position with other Māori colleagues; of course they should be on the marae. I knew the politics; I understood it. At the height of my feminist anger, although I fiercely loved my husband and infant son, I wanted nothing much to do with men.

I felt ashamed at my reaction. After the alarm and shame came another wave: loss. I was losing my closest work friends, and the end of conversations in the tea room, in doorways and corridors, in the photocopying room, in offices and meetings. In those rich conversations, we all grew. We talked about theory; what we were reading; about our kids, parents and partners; about food and health; we discussed our students and we planned new courses. We supported each other, one at a time, through our respective PhDs, and taught each other's classes if needed.

I could have asked Graham if I could relocate as well, to be a part of Māori Education. He may or may not have agreed. Māori calls for solidarity, self-determination or tino rangatiratanga, and strategic separatism were growing in the university and elsewhere. I understood that those tactics were necessary. I assumed that my role, if I had one, was to support Māori initiatives from the 'outside' where, even if I were lonely, I could be staunch.

If Graham or the others had seen me holed up by myself, they might have treated me kindly, though they would probably have thought: toughen up and support the kaupapa, which, in this case, was the politics of Māori collectivity. But no amount of sympathy for their political position could reduce my personal sense of loss. My (Pākehā) head of department had warned me about the risks of being a researcher amongst Māori: 'Your research will never be your own, and you will never be able to be independent.' She was correct, but did not understand that I did not *want* to be an independent researcher-entrepreneur, even though that seemed to be the university's general expectation.

Within a couple of weeks, my friends had gone to their new offices. Despite our physical separation, Kuni and I continued to teach and research and write together. But I missed her daily presence.

———

I was to experience the same ambivalent sadness a few years later, but this time with a different outcome. The government had decided that teacher education in New Zealand was to be led by researchers, so teachers' colleges were assimilated into universities. The university's education department was joined with the Auckland Teachers' College. This reorganisation in 2004 offered me a chance to work more closely with Māori. I asked the Teachers' College Māori head of department if I could be part of the newly created School of Māori Education. No one in that group objected outright to my request. It was not a 'yes', but not a 'no' either. I knew that, sometimes, Māori may appear to be indifferent or even be welcoming, with unhappiness behind the scenes.

It all blew up at a staff meeting. A male colleague stood and spoke vehemently in te reo against a Pākehā presence in the School. I understood enough of what he was saying to realise that, as far as he and some others were concerned, I was not welcome. I sat in my chair, mute and miserable, my eyes downcast. I felt intimidated and humiliated. Then, after a few minutes, an astonishing thing happened. As he spoke, a woman colleague, Tauwehe, suddenly stood up and began to waiata. In a gutsy and resolute manner, she was taking up the right of a senior woman to close down a man's speech with a song. Then she greeted me directly in Māori, and my 'university knowledge', as she called it, saying in English: 'We look forward to you boosting us up.' And that was that. No more was said on the matter.

I wished so much that I could have replied in te reo Māori, thanking her for her generosity, and acknowledging our male colleague for expressing his views. I wanted to explain that I understood the problem he had in accepting a Pākehā in a school of Māori education, and the tension between political self-determination (strictly 'by Māori, for Māori') and an environment of openness to strategic alliances. I wanted to tell him that I would be a staunch ally for Māori. But I could not say these things out loud because I did not have the kīnaki (literally

condiment or relish) of the Māori language to sweeten my
speech or to form my meanings. My bald Pākehā pronounce-
ments would seem arrogant, even patronising, as though I knew
what he thought and what he should think. Instead, I sat in
silence, nodding my miserable gratitude to Tauwehe. Never had
I felt so inadequate to an occasion.

When I tell Pākehā about this event now, they cringe and
call me 'brave' for even being in that situation. I do not see it as
courage because, despite my emotions, the scene as it played
out was not about me. It was about an always-difficult situation
for Māori – a situation for which I have sympathy. I would not
have stayed in the School of Māori Education if I did not have
Māori support. Ultimately, it was for them to decide my place in
that relationship for that moment.

One effect of that denunciation, and Tauwehe's spirited
response, was to reinforce my staunch loyalty to the Māori
group into which I had been welcomed. I had been warned
against the perils of accepting this obligation, but I knew
it was the bedrock of my relationship with Māori, however
complicated that might prove to be.

And it *was* complicated. A group of Māori influential in the
academy continued to assert a form of Māori sovereignty that
remained hostile to Pākehā researchers working with Māori on
Māori topics. Kuni and I both came under pressure, but with a
difference. She was challenged by her Māori peers: 'Why are
you working with a Pākehā? What is wrong with a Māori co-
researcher?' and 'Alison is just using you for her own career.'
I was told quite directly that I was not welcome to work, even
with Māori colleagues, on projects that engaged with kaupapa
Māori theory which, I was reminded, was 'by Māori, for Māori'.

I got it. I did. That was why I often refused to help some

other Pākehā researchers struggling in Māori contexts. I was often approached for assistance by Pākehā, especially overseas white scholars, keen to 'work with Māori communities' or 'get into Māori schools to do some research'. Without long-standing personal links into these places, they were unlikely to be successful, so I would meet them for coffee to explain Linda Tuhiwai Smith's sentence in *Decolonising Methodologies* that 'research' is 'one of the dirtiest words in the indigenous world's vocabulary'.[7] Māori, quite reasonably, I explained, are rarely interested in working with outsiders unless they can see a clear benefit, and can trust the researcher. Some Pākehā researchers are disappointed with my advice; others are grateful that I have solved the mystery of why they have failed to get anyone to return phone calls or turn up to meetings.

I was continuing to teach Māori students, now with new Māori colleagues, particularly Te Kawehau Hoskins from Ngāpuhi. Like Kuni, Te Kawehau had been my PhD student, and I was impressed by her insights and her politics. She always had something truly interesting to say. I quickly came to see her as my teacher, as I had with Kuni. I did not ask her to teach me; I simply spent enough time with her. And I really liked her. We shared an easy familiarity and a sense of humour.

We both noticed that many of our Māori students were wary of reading Pākehā authors, while retaining a hostile focus on Pākehā. They wrote about Pākehā colonisation and racism, Pākehā-caused disadvantage and underachievement, focusing on the wrongs of Pākehā and the Pākehā system of education. Unsurprisingly, they often seemed stuck in anger.

Te Kawehau said to our Māori students: with all your energy and intelligence, and with the time you have studying, why not focus positively on the rich resources in your Māori knowledge and culture, and bring to life a Māori-centred world view? And why not risk reading the best of European philosophers as well, carefully garnering from them theoretical tools to help enrich writing critically from a Māori point of view? She noticed that, although Māori students wrote negatively about Pākehā, they were nonetheless culturally oriented to deeply relational ideas such as mana, and manaakitanga. She asked our students: 'What does this contradiction mean?'

Te Kawehau did not reject the importance of understanding the effects of colonisation, but she offered an alternative to a relentlessly negative positioning of Māori-as-colonised. For her, the most interesting questions centre on mobilising Māori knowledge – not only for the Māori students and their whānau and hapū, but for addressing global questions and for positive human practices. Te Kawehau's approach encouraged me to point out to the students that although te ao Māori and te ao Pākehā – our two worlds – rest on different ontologies and epistemologies (assumptions about the nature of being and knowledge), at the same time, we should not fall into defaulting always to simple binaries. New Zealand's history is not simply a story of bad-coloniser and good-Māori. All of us must study the injustices of New Zealand colonisation, but we must also note that some Pākehā politicians did defend nineteenth-century Māori land rights; that some Pākehā were genuine friends with Māori; that many Pākehā did want justice for Māori; that Māori and Pākehā have formed and continue to form strategic alliances. None of this is said defensively, as special pleading. It is part of a critical education, where complexity is welcomed and embraced rather than avoided.

Teaching complexity is easier said than done. It is risky territory. A simple binary story, as I learned in the heady 1980s, is galvanising in its clarity and its moral force. And the story of colonisation and land loss and language loss is compelling, even energising, in the anger it can generate. But when that story alone dominates, other powerful possibilities for political and social change are diminished. For Māori students, a positive and sustained engagement with te ao Māori can be derailed by understandable rage; as educators, we want to orient those students towards positive Māori possibilities, to *be* Māori. For our Pākehā students, anxiety comes readily in the face of Māori anger and a non-heroic settler history; but we want them to be able to learn about our history, to be open to engagements with Māori, and to *be* Pākehā in all its complications.

Amongst my Māori colleagues there were enough who thought I was useful to a partnership to reduce the sting of criticisms of my work as a Pākehā. Te Kawehau, always keenly intelligent about difficult questions, maintained that 'it is not *what* you are, but *who* you are, that matters most'. I was, as I described it to myself, trying to think in complex ways about being Pākehā as a relational identity. My job was, and still is, to unsettle the idea of who I am – who we Pākehā are, and can be – and to learn how to embrace difficulties rather than trying to resolve them.[8] It remains stimulating work and in it I feel profoundly alive.

The pīwakawaka and the kaumātua

Kuni and I were by now firm friends. Our friendship was not
one of family dinners, or outings, or casual visits to each other's
homes. It was a friendship based on a warm sense of mutual love
and loyalty, and a shared fascination with our research and its
stimulating conversations. Kuni had taken up a position at Te
Whare Wānanga o Awanuiārangi, the Māori tertiary institution
in Whakatāne, but we continued to talk often, both on the
phone and in person when she was in Auckland.

Ours was a friendship not simply between two individuals,
but between a Māori scholar and a Pākehā one. In our working
partnership, we inhabited quite different positions: I was our
writer and she developed our key ideas, teaching me how to
use a Māori lens. She always introduced our joint presenta-
tions with a mihi before my own, rather less knowledgeable,
one. We both knew that, merely by her presence, she gave
me a legitimacy in Māori contexts, protecting me somewhat
from Māori criticism of a Pākehā telling a Māori story, or from
wandering ill-equipped into a Māori setting. For my part, my
skills as a writer and the time I had available meant we could
complete our project (like all Māori women I knew, Kuni always
had impossible demands on her time). We never argued. Kuni
wryly tolerated my Pākehā know-it-all tendencies, remaining
kind and loving towards me, and generous with her knowledge.

One morning in April 2008, I needed her presence in a

very personal way. It was a perfect brisk late autumn day and
I was driving through city streets. On the passenger seat of
my small Toyota was my left breast. It had been removed a few
weeks earlier, together with the 17-millimetre tumour that had
developed in its soft tissue. I had driven alone to a nondescript
building in an industrial part of Auckland, where I was given
a plastic bag inside a brown paper bag. A kind, soft-spoken
man warned me as he handed it over that it would not look like
human flesh because of all the dyes that had been used in the
testing procedures. I hadn't planned to look at it, but it was
thoughtful of him to warn me. I picked up the bag, still cold from
its refrigerated storage, and felt my breast's weight. Something
that had, quite literally, been part of me was now apart from me,
forever separated and, in effect, dead. My breast and I walked
outside into the sunlight and I placed it gently on the car seat,
wondering whether I should strap it in somehow with a seat belt
in case it slid off onto the floor.

At home, I carried the bag down the garden to the place it
was to be buried, under an old plum tree. I set it down, took up a
spade and dug a hole in the rich earth. A pīwakawaka suddenly
appeared, dancing along the tree's lichen-covered branches. It
ducked and dived in close, looking out for disturbed insects. The
bird's loud chirrups sounded like cheeky reassurances. 'E pai
ana! E pai ana!'

Perhaps the bird and I could have done the deed, but I felt a
sudden aching need for some other spiritual help to lay that bag
and its contents into the earth. I sat down. To distract myself for a
moment, I wondered about more earthly things: whether I should
put plastic into the ground. Maybe I should pour out its organic
content into the soil, even if it was poisoned with dyes. But I could
not bring myself to look at that wounded mass of dead flesh.

The little bird, undismayed by the plastic or its paper bag, swooped down towards the interesting object. I began to cry. I did not feel self-pity – more a deep sense of spiritual inadequacy. I did not know what to do. I could have asked the hospital authorities to burn my breast along with other removed breasts, kidneys, bowels and fingers, but I had wanted to take it home for a decent burial. What was a decent burial? Under the plum tree, I sat with the bag, and the pīwakawaka chirruping, waiting for the next move.

I stood up, went inside to get my phone and rang Kuni. Luckily, she was in. 'Help me, Kuni. I am burying my breast.' Kuni did not hesitate. 'Alison, go get a glass of water. I will wait.' I tearfully did as I was told. I filled a glass, took it outside, back to the bird and the bag and the tree. I sat next to the hole in the earth listening for what, at this moment, felt like essential guidance. She was practical. 'Put the bag in the earth. Sprinkle the water.' I put down the phone again, and sprinkled the little grave with water. The bird watched curiously. Kuni calmly spoke the words I wanted in Māori. I did not listen to the words' meanings, I simply felt their reassuring power, and deep softness.

Then, I pushed in some dark earth, tamped it down. It was all over. I picked up the phone: 'Ngā mihi, e hoa. Thanks'. The bird flitted away and was gone. I flicked some water over myself for good measure, repeating a simple act of cleansing that Māori enact when leaving a tapu space.

My sudden decision to call Kuni had surprised me. I had not wanted anyone with me for the burial. And there were other, Pākehā friends I could have called. But I knew that Kuni would give me exactly what I needed, in that moment. I had turned to her, I realised, because she is Māori. Her uncomplicated spiritual connection to the land and all its forces was right for my moment of crisis. She had spoken to me in te reo, a medium we do not usually use with each other, and that language soothed me. She knew instinctively what I was asking of her. And she generously shared a part of it with me.

But there was something else in her words. My own people's spirits – those of the Christian God – do not inhabit this place, for me. I do not feel them. On the other hand, Māori gods – atua – *are* here, for me, somehow. I do not adopt those spiritual connections so much as encounter their forces. It is as though they inhere in the rocks, waterways, skies, birds and trees, the landscapes of Aotearoa. I never feel this same steadying relationship with the land and its creatures when I look out over the mighty canyons of the Blue Mountains in Australia, or the great valleys and forests of the English Lake District, or any of the magnificent rocks, waterways, skies, birds and trees in other countries, no matter how intense their beauty.

I laugh at myself as I write this. To see Māori spirits as distinct from Christian ones is a curious separation, given that forms of Christianity have been alive in Māori communities for almost two hundred years, and were woven into Kuni's karakia. There were no disjunctions for her. She, a lifelong Anglican, seemed to effortlessly hold all these spirits together. I am also grinning ruefully, in a self-mocking way, at an imagined accusation: 'You liberal Pākehā are dial-a-Māori! When it suits, you wheel in a sentimental version of te ao Māori, moulded in your own image.' I understand this denunciation. It is probably true. After all, there I was, burying my breast *alone*. Such a Pākehā! But a person can only act on what they feel is right at any given moment. Kuni's unconditional aroha and her words gave me peace.

By 2011, Kuni and I had finished our book.[1] In the process of
writing it, we had become more deeply engaged with the people
of the north, and the first book generated a second, a biography
of a Ngare Raumati man, Tuai, who had been instrumental in
the establishment of the first school in New Zealand, which was
eventually published in 2017.[2] Kuni and I got into the habit of
travelling to the Bay of Islands to visit historical sites, marae,
schools and community meetings. We listened to stories, and
took opportunities to talk about our research. I inevitably
learned a lot on those trips.

Two memories stand out. Kuni's friend, Teina, invited
Kuni and me to visit her house in a lovely little remote seaside
settlement. Classic old Kiwi baches, each unique, jostled for
space along the foreshore. Caravans were extended with
plywood or corrugated-iron walls, often all painted one colour
to erase the joins of a dwelling cobbled together over years,
growing with one lean-to, then another.

Each bach had a low rough fence around it, marking little
plots of land. As we sat on Teina's porch watching the Pākehā
neighbours' evening barbecue on their front lawn, she told us
this area was her grandfather's tribal land. In the 1940s he had
allowed some Pākehā who travelled down the dusty road to this
remote place by the water, to set up their tents and caravans
for the summer. They loved it so much they came back, year
after year, and, now into the second and third generation, had
added bits and pieces to make quite comfortably solid baches.
They paid a few dollars a year to the hapū for their possies
which, each summer, became crowded with their friends' tents
and caravans and cars. I asked Teina whether she minded this

haphazard expansion and the summer invasion. She said she did not much like it, and that her family made very little money from the sites. But how could she change the arrangement, and upset the Pākehā that her grandfather had allowed to stay on the land? It had been her grandfather's decision, and Teina accepted his manaaki towards the Pākehā. Her other family members also remembered the old man's generosity, and were loath to challenge it. I was troubled by Teina's ambivalence; I felt much more rejecting of the interlopers. But it was not my land, or my grandfather, or the manaaki of my people at stake.

Teina's logic reflected the complexity of her (non-)identity as an individual. She, and her family, were profoundly inseparable from her tūpuna, and her hapū. She was not an individual in any western sense of that word. I recalled a student pointing out a verse where a Ngāti Porou speaker equates himself with his tribe, referring to his iwi in the first-person singular:

He pū! He pū!
Nā te pū i mate ai au
a Ngāti Porou i a Ngāpuhi
Mehemea he taiaha ki te taiaha
Kāore i mate au

O' the musket! O' the musket!
T'was by the musket that I
Ngāti Porou was killed by Ngāpuhi
If it had been with traditional weapons
I would not have been defeated.[3]

The speaker naturally understood himself ('au') in collective terms; he was the embodied presence of his people and vice versa. Similarly, an article by Ngāpuhi scholar Patu Hohepa on

Ngāpuhi is titled 'My Musket, My Missionary, My Mana', but
he is not writing about *his* musket; he is writing as a Ngāpuhi.
Such a strong sense of relationship with others, including
objects (understood in Western thought as inanimate), is also
commonly heard in the saying 'Ko au te awa; ko te awa ko au'
(I am the river and the river is me). In this sense, the individual
becomes always a part of something else, and only exists *in
relation* to something else.[4]

Another memory still reddens my Pākehā cheeks. I was
up at Waitangi for a Tribunal hearing in 2010. I met an old
man, a kaumātua, who, hearing about my research interests,
generously related a story about his Ngāpuhi ancestor Hongi
Hika. He told me proudly that when Hongi Hika travelled
to England in 1820, he became the first Māori to see the
greatest ariki of the Pākehā, King George IV. Hongi Hika, he
told me, using only his taiaha that he carried with him from
New Zealand, had alone defeated three of the King's best
swordsmen in a battle. This feat earned him an audience with
the King, and led to an enduring relationship between Ngāpuhi
and the British Crown, reflected in the Treaty with Queen
Victoria.

I had studied Hongi Hika's visit to England and I knew
that he did not fight any soldiers to earn access to the King.
Indeed, King George had been openly interested in meeting
this exotic visitor. I decided to tell the kaumātua the correct
story. 'That is not quite right …' I started enthusiastically. I felt
my new acquaintance bristle. I was pointing at him! He slapped
my hand down with a quick firm gesture. I had insulted this
mild and charming man; I had challenged his mana. Not only
was pointing at him extremely rude, but, also unforgivably,
I had directly questioned his knowledge of his own tupuna. I

had been in enough hui over the years, and listened to enough whaikōrero, to know that Māori generally avoid directly contradicting each other, they scrupulously uphold the rights of others to tell their own stories. And – significantly – Māori approaches to the past differ from my own. For this kaumātua, the story of Hongi Hika's bravery illustrated his ancestor's mana and his legendary fighting abilities. The story was the thing; it spoke eloquently of Hongi Hika's nature and skills. For me, as a Pākehā, history was a different beast. It was made up of verified facts, not illustrative events embellished to tell a wider story about character and power.

I noticed that Pākehā accounts were often ignored out of hand. I found few Māori in the north who read published histories of the region; when I recommended Anne Salmond's excellent books, I was told firmly 'we have our own histories'. I think this response was more a defence than a rejection; Pākehā accounts fail to highlight the stories of most interest. I remembered Patu Hohepa's view on accounts of the past. He stated that 'historical absolutes, this striving for objectivity, has no central place in Māori narrative, where the past and the future are swirling spirals of time, with events and people interacting with the presence of the narrator'.[5]

Always, the presence of the speaker, the living context. The person with whom the listeners, and the topic, have a relationship. I thought about Koro Dewes' comment about Māori learning: 'A face seen,' he said, 'is an argument understood.'[6] Books carry disembodied words, but real people can be known and collectively evaluated, and their words absorbed in the context of a crowd or a conversation. How an argument is understood depends on how the 'face seen' conducts herself. A Māori speaker has many hurdles to overcome: her whakapapa,

her genealogy, will affect her reputation; her education,
her university degrees, may be seen to have reduced her
Māori-ness; and she may be seen as too young to have a mature
viewpoint. A Pākehā face may provide fewer, or more, barriers
between herself and Māori listeners. Her Pākehā whakapapa
means she knows little, or a lot; her education, ditto, depending
on the attitude of the listeners. She has only face value. As an
unknown quantity, she is judged on her āhua (demeanour),
her Māori supporters, her usefulness to the collective, and her
story's connection to what Māori already know – and, often, her
sense of humour.

The old man who slapped my hand that day was delivering
a well-earned reprimand. This was not his people's way of
remembering, and his story was the one they loved and
repeated. Realising all this in a mortifying flash, I apologised.
He looked at me calmly from under the worn brim of his hat: yet
another impolite know-it-all Pākehā. I saw myself suddenly as
uncivilised, a term long used to describe and criticise Māori and
other indigenous peoples. He smiled graciously, and we parted
warmly. But I went away smarting, wishing that I had simply
listened. Defaulting, when I was excited, to my own unthinking
tendency to 'get to the truth' (that is, the story that interested
me) had simply caused offence.

I kept returning to ideas of *relationality*. Relationships
seemed always to be at the heart of all my engagements with
Māori and Māori things, and at the heart of Māori understandings of the world. I thought about how Māori profoundly
understood and understand the world as a series of never-
ending, never-resolved relationships – between people, objects,
time, space and on and on. I had come to realise that for Māori,
boundaries do not contain absolutes. As Anne Salmond put

it, for Māori the world is not 'a singular entity, composed of arrays of bounded entities in different realms and on different scales' as it tends to be in dominant forms of Western thought.[7] Rather, boundaries are conceived of as thresholds, and it is the relationship *between* things rather than things *themselves* that have what she calls 'ontological primacy' – that is, *relationships* between people, and between people and things, are the foundation of Māori commonsense knowledge and encounters in the world. It is in the space between us as we face each other where everything happens, where there is energy of all sorts – the complex, fluid, shifting site occupied by the hyphen in Māori–Pākehā engagements.[8]

When you think in living relational terms, you can't find solace in *solutions*. Solutions suggest that everything is sorted. As a university professor, now, I try to steer my students away from a search for solutions. They often resist. Whether they are Māori or Pākehā, they want to 'save' Māori, end social problems, find the true nature of 'Māori success', come up with five recommendations for practice. But taking relationality seriously throws into disarray our sincere dreams for answers and end points – and our assumption that, one day, we will wake up and *all will be well*. Relationships are never like that. They are contingent, fluid and always on the move, always in the process of being and becoming something. In the end, the most important things are ineffable, unexplainable, difficult, and sometimes even contradictory.

––––––

Back at my Waitangi hotel room, the night after my excruciating reprimand from the kaumātua, I recalled Pākehā historian

Michael King's account of writing a book about Te Puea, a famous Māori leader. King talked for many hours over many days with Te Puea's husband, Rawiri Tumokai, and reported that the latter 'lived for my visits and seemed bereft and uncomprehending when they had to become less frequent. I was writing a book; he was conducting an intense relationship.'[9] That heartbreaking sentence reminded me, yet again, of the centrality of sustained relationships at the beating heart of all close engagements between Māori and Pākehā, whether happy or combative. I wondered if I had killed off any hope of a relationship with my new acquaintance in the old hat, but I suspected not.

I thought about the fact that many Māori, including my late colleague, Professor Ranginui Walker, draw attention to the eternal words of Rewi Maniapoto at the battle of Ōrākau in 1864, during the New Zealand Wars when the Governor's troops were taking Waikato lands: 'Ka whawhai tonu ahau ki a koe, ake ake ake.' Whawhai means 'to fight'. This phrase is often translated as 'I will fight/struggle against you for ever and ever and ever.' It could equally be seen as 'I will fight/struggle *with* you for ever and ever and ever.' As New Zealanders, we are all in that eternal struggle, whether we like it or not. And we all create the nature of that struggle; it is our engagement and our challenge. I feel grateful that Māori are up for civil long-term engagement. The question arising for us Pākehā and other non-Māori is how to engage positively and with justice in that relationship with Māori.

The following day was the Waitangi Tribunal hearing of land claims from the northern tribes, Te Paparahi o Te Raki, which Kuni and I and some others had come to witness. Kuni and I had put in a submission, based on our research in the north. The hearing was to be on the Waitangi waterfront and a large crowd was expected, so I would need to be early to get a seat. I stayed up late that night chatting with my friends, and eventually got to bed at midnight. I had told Kuni to go on ahead in the morning and I would catch up. I slept fitfully, disturbed by dreams. My alarm did not go off. When I woke the sun was glistening on the sparkling Bay of Islands waters, and I knew I was late.

I looked as I hurried alone along the Waitangi beachfront road for the tail end of an ope, a group entering the marae. Everything would be all right.

Glossary

A glossary of Māori and Pacific language words used in the text without translation. The meanings given here are appropriate to this book.

ariki	high chief
ātea	courtyard in front of a meeting house
atua	supernatural being, god
haka	posture dance with chant
hapū	subtribe, tribal group
hongi	traditional greeting by pressing noses
hui	meeting, gathering
iwi	tribe
kaiako	teacher
kaikōrero	speaker
kāinga	village
kapa haka	Māori performing arts
karakia	prayer
kaumātua	an elder
kaupapa	topic, purpose
kōrero	speech, talk
kuia	female elder
kura	school, especially a Māori-language school
mana	prestige, status
manaaki, manaakitanga	hospitality
mana whenua	authority over land
marae	meeting house complex
maunga	mountain
mihi	acknowledgement, greeting
moko kauae	chin tattoo worn by women
mokopuna	grandchild, grandchildren

ope	group of people
paepae	orators' bench on a marae
Pākehā	New Zealander of European descent
palangi	white person
pāua	abalone
poi	light ball on string used in performance, usually by women
pou	carved post
pounamu	greenstone, jade
pōwhiri	ceremony of welcome
pūkana	dilating of the eyes when performing haka and waiata
rangatira	chief
rua	two
tahi	one
taiaha	long wooden weapon
tangi, tangihanga	funeral ceremony
taonga	treasure
tapu	sacred, restricted
te reo Māori	the Māori language
tikanga	traditions, customs
tohunga	priest, expert
toru	three
tukutuku	decorative woven panelling
tūpāpaku	dead body
tupuna	ancestor
tūpuna	ancestors
waiata	song, to sing
waka	canoe
wānanga	institution of higher learning
whaea	mother, aunt; term of respect for a woman
whaikōrero	formal speech
whakapapa	genealogy
whare	house
wharenui	meeting house

Endnotes

Preface

1 Annabel Mikaere, 'Racism in Contemporary Aotearoa: A Pākehā
   Problem', in *Colonising Myths, Māori Realities: He Rukuruku Whakaaro*,
   Huia, Wellington, 2011, p.119.

2 Michael King, *Being Pakeha: An Encounter with New Zealand and the
   Maori Renaissance*, Hodder and Stoughton, Auckland, 1985; Michael King
   (ed.), *Pakeha: The Quest for Identity in New Zealand*, Penguin, Auckland,
   1991; Michael King, *Being Pakeha Now: Reflections and Recollections of a
   White Native*, Penguin, Auckland, 1999.

3 Quoted in Russell Baillie, 'Culture Hero: Peter Wells, 1950–2019', *New
   Zealand Listener*, 9 March 2019, www.noted.co.nz/currently/profiles/
   peter-wells-culture-hero-1950-2019 (accessed 1 May 2019).

4 King, *Being Pakeha*, p.7.

5 Ibid., pp.9–13.

2. Ghosts and arrivals

1 'Kiekie – Freycinetia banksii', The Meaning of Trees, https://
   meaningoftrees.com/2016/04/10/kiekie-freycinetia-banksii (accessed 4
   May 2017).

2 Because many tribes have lived in Tāmaki, there are numerous
   explanations for the origin of its name. See Rāwiri Taonui, 'Tāmaki tribes
   – Tribal history and places', Te Ara – the Encyclopedia of New Zealand,
   www.TeAra.govt.nz/en/tamaki-tribes/page-1 (accessed 6 June 2018).

3 M.H. Wynyard, *The History of One Tree Hill, the Volcanic Mountain Known
   to the Māori People as 'Maungakiekie'*, Wilson and Horton, Auckland,
   1903.

4 In fact, One Tree Hill/Maungakiekie was a public reserve, added to the
   adjacent Cornwall Park that was gifted to the city in 1901 by John Logan
   Campbell, to make a large public park.

3. Learning to stand upright

1   *Report of the Waitangi Tribunal on the Orakei Claim*, Waitangi Tribunal, Wellington, 1987.

2   S. Te Huia Wilson, 'Hape (Rakataura) Settles Puketapapa', manuscript ref. no. MNP MS 24, South Auckland Research Centre, Archives New Zealand.

3   *Auckland Star*, 12 September 1953.

4   *Meet New Zealand*, Historical Branch of the Department of Internal Affairs, Wellington, 1942, pp.15, 20–21, 'Meet New Zealand guide', NZHistory, https://nzhistory.govt.nz/media/interactive/meet-new-zealand-guide (accessed 6 June 2017).

5   Thomas Bevan, 'The Wairau Massacre, June 17th, 1843 – Proceedings between Natives and Surveyors', in *The Reminiscences of An Old Colonist*, Otaki Mail, Ōtaki, 1908, p.52. Also Paul Moon, *FitzRoy: Governor in Crisis 1843–1845*, David Ling, Auckland, 2000, p.131.

4. Finding boundaries

1   Naomi Mitchison, *Presenting Other People's Children*, Paul Hamlyn, London, 1961, p.94.

5. Tricky memories

1   Maori Postal Sunday School movement. See 'History of MPA', Maori Postal Aotearoa, www.maoripostal.co.nz/history-of-mpa (accessed 10 December 2019).

6. Māori on the front lawn

1   In 1999 the Waitangi Tribunal had acknowledged the injustice of the loss of some 245,000 acres of Ngāti Awa tribal lands: Waitangi Tribunal, *Ngati Awa Raupatu Report (Wai 46)*, GP Publications, Wellington, 1999.

2   See also Anton van der Wouden, 'Flourmilling in the Eastern Bay of Plenty', *Historical Review*, 32 (1984), pp.73–89; Anton van der Wouden, 'Maori Shipowners and Pakeha Shipbuilders in the Bay of Plenty 1840–1860', *Historical Review*, 33 (1985), pp.90–100.

7. Two friends

1   Principal's Report, *Te Waka Kura*, VIII, Whakatane High School, Whakatāne, 1967, p.13.

8. Area returned to the Natives

1 Text from poster in the author's possession; attributed to e.e. cummings.

2 Gerard Manley Hopkins, 'Pied Beauty', in James Reeves, *Selected Poems of Gerard Manley Hopkins*, Heinemann, London, 1953, p.24.

3 James K. Baxter, 'East Coast Journey', in J.E. Weir (ed.), *Collected Poems*, Oxford University Press, Wellington, 1980, p.273.

4 Ngāti Ranginui is the iwi. The Ngāti Ranginui hapū at the Bethlehem pā by the harbour, at the end of Bethlehem Road, is Ngāti Hangarau, and at the other local pā, near the Wairoa River, is Ngāti Kahu.

5 Letter from Tīmoti Tutauanui, *Ngā Hapū o Ngāti Ranginui and Trustees of the Nga Hapu Ranginui Settlement and The Crown: Deed of Settlement of Historical Claims*, 21 June 2012, p.15, www.govt.nz/assets/Documents/OTS/Ngati-Ranginui/Ngati-Ranginui-Deed-of-Settlement-21-June-2012.pdf (accessed 9 April 2020).

6 Ibid., pp.22, 24.

7 bid., pp.33–34.

8 Sylvia Ashton-Warner, *Teacher*, Penguin, Harmondsworth, 1966, p.35.

9 Ibid., p.19.

10 I subsequently wrote a number of articles about Sylvia Ashton-Warner, and co-edited a book about her: Alison Jones and Sue Middleton (eds), *The Kiss and the Ghost: Sylvia Ashton-Warner and New Zealand*, Sense Publications, Rotterdam: NZCER Press, Wellington, 2009. See also Alison Jones, 'Sex, Fear and Pedagogy: Sylvia Ashton-Warner's Infant Room', in J.P. Robertson and C. McConaghy (eds), *Provocations: Sylvia Ashton-Warner and Excitability in Education*, Peter Lang, New York, 2006, pp.15–32.

9. Impossible love

1 Lyman Tower Sargent, 'The Ohu Movement', *New Zealand Studies*, 6, 3 (November 1996), pp.18–22, p.18.

2 Donna Awatere Huata, *My Journey*, Seaview Press, Auckland, 1996, p.32.

10. Middle-class olives, and revolution

1 Vincent O'Malley, Bruce Stirling and Wally Penetito, *The Treaty of Waitangi Companion*, Auckland University Press, Auckland, 2010, p.297. Cited from a submission to the Human Rights Commission, 1979. 'Hori' (George) is a racist term for a Māori man.

2 Ranginui Walker, *Ka Whawhai Tonu Mātou. Struggle Without End*, Penguin, Auckland, 2004, p.222.

3   Margie Thomson, *A Proud Herstory: A Celebration of the Auckland Women's Centre, 1975–2010*, Auckland Women's Centre, Auckland, 2010.

4   Camille Guy, Alison Jones and Gay Simpkin, 'From Piha to Postfeminism', *Sites*, 20 (Autumn 1990), p.9.

5   These memories are recorded in Guy, Jones and Simpkin, 'From Piha to Postfeminism', pp.11–12.

6   Alison Jones, Annabel Fagan, Carole Stewart, Elizabeth Dowling, Nancy Peterson, Pilar Alba and Rebecca Evans, 'Towards Revolution', *Bitches, Witches and Dykes*, 1, 1 (August 1980), p.1.

7   Minutes by Carole Stewart, 'Our Collective Process!', *Bitches, Witches and Dykes*, 1, 1 (August 1980), p.1.

8   Ripeka Evans, 'Black Women's Manifesto', *Black Forum* in *Bitches, Witches and Dykes*, 1, 2 (December 1980), p.12.

9   'From the collective (without consensus)', *Bitches, Witches and Dykes*, 1, 4 (November 1981), p.1.

10   See for instance, 'Maori Radicals and the Pakeha Left: How Much in Common?', *The Republican*, July 1982, pp.13–16; 'Donna Awatere & Maori Sovereignty – A Marxist View', *The Republican*, December 1982, pp.7–16; 'Maori Sovereignty and Decolonisation', *The Republican*, February 1983, p.2; 'Why the Treaty Is a Fraud', *The Republican*, February 1983, p.3. *The Republican* newsletter ran to eighty-five issues, from about 1974 to 1995.

11   Donna Awatere, *Maori Sovereignty*, Auckland, Broadsheet, 1984, p.56.

12   Ibid., p.14.

13   Ibid., p.43.

14   Gay Simpkin, 'Women for Aotearoa: Feminism and Māori Sovereignty', *Hecate*, 20, 2 (1994), pp.226–38, p.227.

15   Alison Jones and seven others, letter to *Broadsheet*, January/February 1983, p.2; Jill Newell, Alison Jones, Joce Jesson, Gay Simpkin, Camille Guy and Jenefer Wright, 'Pakeha Women Respond to Maori Sovereignty', *Broadsheet*, June 1983, pp.16–18, 37–39; Camille Guy, 'Getting Away from Racist Guilt', *Broadsheet*, September 1986, pp.30–32; Alison Jones and Camille Guy, 'Radical Feminism in New Zealand: From Piha to Newtown', in Rosemary du Plessis and Phillida Bunkle (eds), *Feminist Voices*, Oxford University Press, Auckland, 1992, pp.300–16.

16   Awatere, *Maori Sovereignty*, p.15.

17   'I look at it [the term white hatred] now and have a mild sense of *whakama*, of shame. I do not believe that non-Maori hate Maori. But [...] I will say that white behaviour to Maori in those days had the same effect

as hatred [...] The words "white hatred" were wrong, quite wrong.' Donna Awatere Huata, *My Journey*, Seaview Press, Auckland, 1996, pp.80, 94.

18   Awatere, *Maori Sovereignty*, p.66.

19   Ibid., p.32.

20   Ibid., p.52.

11. Light on the kūmara garden

1   A chi rho (XP) symbol is an early form of the name Jesus Christ. It superimposes the first two letters of the Greek word for Christ.

2   'Thou art indeed just, Lord, if I contend.' *Gerard Manley Hopkins: Poems and Prose*, Penguin Classics, London, 1985.

3   For instance, Tūmatauenga (god of war and mankind) stands as a strong straight toko, Tāwhirimātea (god of wind and storm) as a corkscrew, Tangaroa (god of oceans) as zig-zag waves, Rongo (god of cultivated plants, especially kūmara) as a series of swellings. See Fig. 27 in D.R. Simmons and Te Riria, 'Whakapakoko Rakau: Godsticks', *Records of the Auckland Institute and Museum*, 20 December 1983, pp.123–45.

4   My PhD, completed in 1986, was published in 1991. Alison Jones, *At School I've Got a Chance: Culture/Privilege: Pacific Islands and Pakeha Girls at School,* Dunmore Press, Palmerston North, 1991.

5   Richard A. Benton, *Can the Maori Language Survive?*, Maori Unit, New Zealand Council for Educational Research, Wellington, an address prepared for the Conference of University Teachers of Maori Studies and Maori Language, Victoria University of Wellington, August 1978.

6   *Matua Rautia: The Report on the Kōhanga Reo Claim* (Wai 2336), Waitangi Tribunal, Wellington, 2012, p.20, www.waitangitribunal.govt.nz/assets/Documents/Publications/WT-Matua-Rautia-Report-on-the-Kohanga-Reo-claim.pdf (accessed December 2018).

7   Thanks to Jenny Page for drawing my attention to an unpublished report by Waiora Port titled 'A Brief History of the Establishment of Our Ritimana Kohanga Reo', n.d. (1985?).

12. Wānanga

1   William Weaver Tomlinson, *A Comprehensive Guide to Northumberland* (1889), quoted in 'The Cheviot Photo', Guide to Britain's Hills & Mountains, www.themountainguide.co.uk/photos/the-cheviot-2879122.htm (accessed 20 January 2019).

13. A surprising whakapapa

1   My thanks to Andrew Hamilton Buchanan and Neal Harkness Buchanan.

2   Andrew Buchanan to his sister, probably Elizabeth Sheriff, 26 March 1864, reproduced in Andrew Hamilton Buchanan and Neal Harkness Buchanan, *Andrew Buchanan of Chingford 1807–1877*, Hazard Press, Christchurch, 1995, pp.17–20.

3   Private Act Anno 26, Georgii III 1785, *The Laws of Jamaica: 1760–1792*, A. Aikman, printer to the King's Most Excellent Majesty, 1802.

4   Vincent O'Malley, *The Great War for New Zealand: Waikato 1800–2000*, Bridget Williams Books, Wellington, 2016, p.16. See also 'Andrew Buchanan of Chingford and Patearoa', in Robert Fulton, *Medical Practice in the Early Days*, Otago Daily Times and Witness Newspapers Co., 1922, pp.82–89.

5   In March 1864 Andrew wrote that his sons-in-law, based normally in Auckland, were 'with the troops who are at the seat of war' against the Kīngitanga forces in the Waikato. Letter to 'My dear Sister', 26 March 1864, in Andrew Buchanan and Neal Buchanan, *Andrew Buchanan of Chingford 1807–1877*, p.19.

6   'New Zealand', *New Zealand Gazette and Wellington Spectator*, 25 April 1840, reprinted from the *Hobart Town Advertiser*, https://paperspast. natlib.govt.nz/newspapers/NZGWS18400425.2.10 (accessed 3 January 2020).

7   'Letters from Captain Robertson of the Barque "Samuel Winter". Dated Kororarika [sic] Nov 10, 1839', *The New Zealand Journal*, Saturday 01 August, 1840, p.181, https://library.huttcity.mebooks.co.nz/text/ NZJournal18400801/t1-g1-t14-front-d2.html (accessed 28 October 2018).

8   Ibid.

9   Ibid.

10 Ibid.

11 'New Zealand', *New Zealand Gazette* and *Wellington Spectator*, 25 April 1840.

12 Ibid.

13 Buchanan had been appointed to a seat on the New Zealand Legislative Council (the Upper House) in 1862. See Andrew Buchanan and Neal Buchanan, *Andrew Buchanan of Chingford 1807–1877*, p.25, citing Fulton, *Medical Practice in the Early Days*, 1922.

14 William Baldwin and Jim Sullivan, *Tom Hungerford: A Story of the Early Days in the Otago Goldfields*, New Zealand Colonial Texts series, University of Otago, Dunedin, 2011, p.100.

15   Neal Harkness Buchanan and Andrew Hamilton Buchanan (eds), *Andrew Buchanan Diaries, 1865, 1873*, Hazard Press, Christchurch, 1997, p.66.

16   Ibid., p.41.

17   Ibid., p.66.

18   Andrew Buchanan, Friday 18 August 1865 entry, Neal Buchanan and Andrew Buchanan (eds), *Andrew Buchanan Diaries, 1865, 1873*, p.30.

19   Ibid., p.18.

20   New Zealand Settlements Act 1863 – 'An Act to Enable the Governor to Establish Settlements for Colonisation in the Northern Island of New Zealand', 3 December 1863, NZLII, www.nzlii.org/nz/legis/hist_act/nzsa186327v1863n8377 (accessed 27 February 2019).

14. Risky territory

1   J.L. Nicholas, *Narrative of a Voyage to New Zealand, Performed in the Years 1814 and 1815, in Company with the Rev. Samuel Marsden, Principal Chaplain of New South Wales*, vol. 1, James Black and Son, London, 1817, p.181.

2   The Pākehā historian Anne Salmond says something similar about her learning about Māori things: 'I learnt as much through the skin, through the soles of my feet. Through sleeping on the marae, through being caught up, sometimes, in really emotional situations because you love people.' Quoted in Diana Wichtel, An Interview with Dame Anne Salmond, *New Zealand Listener*, 21 January 2012, pp.19–21.

3   Michael King, *Being Pakeha: An Encounter with New Zealand and the Maori Renaissance*, Hodder and Stoughton, Auckland, 1985, p.112.

4   Alison Jones, 'The Limits of Cross-cultural Dialogue: Pedagogy, Desire and Absolution in the Classroom', *Educational Theory*, 49, 3 (Summer 1999), pp.299–316, p.302.

15. A broken hill

1   Vincent O'Malley, *The Great War for New Zealand: Waikato 1800–2000*, Bridget Williams Books, Wellington, 2016.

2   In 2017 a new motorway replaced this part of the highway. The motorway heading south runs further to the side of the site, and commemorative pou have been placed on the battle site, visible to the left of the motorway on the hillside.

3   Waitangi Tribunal, *Finding of the Waitangi Tribunal on the Manukau Claim (Wai 8)*, Government Printer, Wellington, 1985, p.13ff.

4   John Featon, *The Waikato War, 1863–4*, 1879, p.22, www.enzb.auckland.

ac.nz/docs/Featon/pdf/feat1000.pdf (accessed 19 July 2019). See also O'Malley, *The Great War*, p.208.

5   James Belich, 'Cameron, Duncan Alexander', Dictionary of New Zealand Biography, Te Ara – the Encyclopedia of New Zealand, https://teara.govt. nz/en/biographies/1c2/cameron-duncan-alexander (accessed 18 July 2019).

6   See Alison Jones and Kuni Jenkins, *He Kōrero: Words Between Us – First Māori–Pākehā Conversations on Paper*, Huia, Wellington, 2011, pp.89–102.

7   Linda Tuhiwai Smith, *Decolonising Methodologies: Research and Indigenous Peoples*, Zed Books, London, 1999, p.1.

8   I wrote about the idea of embracing such struggle in Alison Jones, 'Dangerous Liaisons: Pākehā, Kaupapa Māori, and Educational Research', *New Zealand Journal of Educational Studies*, 47, 2 (2012), pp.101–13.

16. The pīwakawaka and the kaumātua

1   Alison Jones and Kuni Jenkins, *He Kōrero: Words Between Us – First Māori–Pākehā Conversations on Paper*, Huia, Wellington, 2011.

2   Alison Jones and Kuni Kaa Jenkins, *Tuai: A Traveller in Two Worlds*, Bridget Williams Books, Wellington, 2017.

3   Thanks to Rewa Paewai for drawing this to my attention. Cited in Monty Soutar, 'I Te Wa i a Mea', MA thesis, Massey University, Palmerston North, 1991, p.82.

4   I find this article useful in thinking about the individual and relationality: Anne Salmond, 'Ontological Quarrels: Indigeneity, Exclusion and Citizenship in a Relational World', *Anthropological Theory*, 12, 2 (2012), pp.115–41.

5   Patu Hohepa, 'My Musket, My Missionary, My Mana', in Alex Calder, Jonathan Lamb and Bridget Orr (eds), *Voyages and Beaches: Pacific Encounters*, University of Hawaii Press, Honolulu, 1999, pp.180–81.

6   Michael King, *Being Pakeha: An Encounter with New Zealand and the Maori Renaissance*, Hodder and Stoughton, Auckland, 1985, p.110.

7   Salmond, 'Ontological Quarrels', p.124.

8   Alison Jones, 'Rethinking Collaboration: Working the Indigene-Colonizer Hyphen', in N. Denzin, Y. Lincoln and L.T. Smith (eds), *Handbook of Critical Indigenous Methodologies*, Sage, New York, 2008, pp.471–86.

9   King, *Being Pakeha*, pp.136–37.

Acknowledgements

I thank all those who, visibly and invisibly, are in my narrative.

Friends and teachers and others who appear in this book: Te Kawehau Hoskins, Kuni Kaa Jenkins, Maria Te Amo, Jackie Haimona, Rāhera Ohia, Donna Awatere Huata, Ripeka Evans, Linda Tuhiwai Smith, Graham Hingangaroa Smith, Tauwehe Tamati, Buster Black (Thomas Pihama), Bunny Thompson, Rewa Paewai, the Hana family, Rowan Tautari, Akarana, Mere, Teina, Mrs Florence Maaka, Dun Mihaka, Colonel Awatere, the girls of Bollard Girls' Home, my teacher and classmates of Te Pūtaketanga at Te Whare Wānanga o Aotearoa, James K. Baxter, Vivienne Smith, Rev. Glad Stiles, John Chaplin and the Chaplin family, Sylvia Ashton-Warner, Mr Kingsley-Smith, Lesley Phillips, Joce and Bruce Jesson, Malcolm Francis, Anne Salmond, Charmaine Pountney, Kerry Wilson, Koloni (who I hope is a happy adult), my old friends from Women for Aotearoa, and from *Bitches Witches and Dykes*.

Other friends, critics, teachers: Margie Thomson, Margie Wetherell (who got me started), my kaumātua and mentor Te Warihi Hetaraka, Camille Guy, Sailau Suaalii, Stephen Turner, Dame Joan Metge, Deb Rewiri, Liz McKinley, Ngahuia Te Awekotuku, Kīmai Tocker, Dave Fa'avae, Lincoln Dam, Hazel Petrie, Avril Bell, Georgina Stewart, Judith Simon, Vikki Demant, Hēmi Dale, Helene Connor, Melinda Webber, Rose Yukich, Frances Hancock, Glenn Colquhoun, Jim Marshall, Stuart McNaughton, Jenny Lee Morgan, Leonie Pihama, David

Stenhouse, Miss Chatfield and Mrs McKenzie my primary school teachers, Mr Sullivan my secondary school English teacher.

As always, my family: my sons Finn McCahon Jones and Frey McCahon Jones, and Emma and Alfie. My niece Sophie Whittle Jones. My mother Ruth Jones and her large family, especially her half-sisters Monica and Charlotte, and her half-brother Mark. My father Basil Jones, and his brother, Peter Jones. My sisters and brothers, Gillian, Richard, Olive and Garrick. My ex-husband William McCahon, his parents Colin and Anne McCahon, and his sister Tora (Victoria) Carr. My many cousins, especially Andrew Buchanan and Vicki Graham.

Countless others, whose names I do not know, who had a remembered impact on my life, including the man outside Dannevirke Hospital, the Northland kaumātua in the hat, the kuia who sat along the Strand in Whakatāne, the guy who handed me my breast in a plastic bag.

I am grateful to the Faculty Research Development Fund of the University of Auckland for support, and to Margie Thomson and Jane Parkin for their writing advice and editing. My thanks to the team at BWB and to Bridget Williams for her editorial suggestions.

Finally, my love and gratitude to my husband and editor Peter Calder.

Ka nui taku aroha ki a koutou katoa.